TRACING YOUR WELSH ANCESTORS

FAMILY HISTORY FROM PEN & SWORD

TRACING YOUR WELSH ANCESTORS

A Guide for Family Historians

Beryl Evans

Published in association with
The National Library of Wales, Aberystwyth

Pen & Sword
FAMILY HISTORY

First published in Great Britain in 2015
PEN & SWORD FAMILY HISTORY
an imprint of
Pen & Sword Books Ltd
47 Church Street, Barnsley
South Yorkshire,
S70 2AS

ISBN 978 1 84884 359 2

Typeset in Palatino and Optima by CHIC GRAPHICS

Printed and bound in England by
CPI Group (UK), Croydon, CR0 4YY

Pen & Sword Books Ltd incorporates the imprints of Pen & Sword
Archaeology, Atlas, Aviation, Battleground, Discovery, Family History,
History, Maritime, Military, Naval, Politics, Railways, Select, Social History,
Transport, True Crime, Claymore Press, Frontline Books, Leo Cooper,
Praetorian Press, Remember When, Seaforth Publishing and Wharncliffe.

For a complete list of Pen & Sword titles please contact
PEN & SWORD BOOKS LTD
47 Church Street, Barnsley, South Yorkshire, S70 2AS, England
E-mail: enquiries@pen-and-sword.co.uk
Website: www.pen-and-sword.co.uk

CONTENTS

In memory of my special nephew,
Harri Rhys Rattray
2000–2013

ACKNOWLEDGEMENTS

Many people have helped and guided me whilst writing this book and I am grateful to them all, with special thanks to Simon Fowler for his patience and kind words whilst reading the text over the years. My greatest thanks go to the staff at the National Library of Wales; without the support, encouragement and resources made available to me, it would not have been possible to complete the work. The Library has also provided me with many images from its collections, from which I have tried to choose examples from all over Wales, not only from my home county of Ceredigion.

Last, but by no means least, thank you to Emlyn – my husband – and my daughters Caryl and Elan, for their continued support. A special mention goes to my granddaughters Elan Lois and Popi Mai; I'm hoping that all my family history research will not be in vain.

LIST OF ILLUSTRATIONS

1. A selection of items that can be found whilst searching for family records. (Author's collection)
2. A collection of nineteenth-century memorial cards. (Author's collection)
3. A collection of photographs that have been kept in the family. (Author's collection)
4. The pedigree of John Salisbury, compiled in 1627 by Jacob Chaloner. (NLW, Peniarth Ms 475G)
5. Gravestones at Gwynfil Calvinistic Methodist Chapel, Llangeitho, Ceredigion. (Author's collection)
6. An example of the use of the patronymic naming system in burials, 1698, Llangelynnin parish, Caernarfonshire. (NLW, BTs Llangelynnin)
7. A road sign showing the use of both Welsh and English. (Author's collection)
8. Screenshot of the National Library of Wales website. (NLW)
9. The birth certificate of Thomas William, Eglwysilan, Glamorganshire, 1857. (NLW, Bute D161/7)
10. The marriage certificate of David Lloyd George and Margaret Owen, Pencaenewydd Chapel, Caernarfonshire. (NLW, Ms 20477C)
11. The death certificate of David Griffith Davies, Pontypridd, 1887. (NLW, Shadrach and Lewis Pryce Papers 71)
12. 1841 Census for Yskirfechan township, Merthyr Cynog parish, Breconshire, which shows the ages of the householders rounded down to the nearest 5 years. (TNA, HO 107/1368/13, p.6)
13. 1891 census for the parish of Ysbytty Ystwyth, Cardiganshire. The form shows a 'W' in the first column, which indicates that

Chapter 1

STARTING YOUR RESEARCH

The questions I am most often asked in relation to family history research are: 'How do I start?' or 'Where do I start?' More often than not, my answer is, 'With yourself!' It is surprising how much we already know about our families without realizing. Make a note of all the names, dates and events you are certain of, concerning not only your immediate family, but also extended family. Start with yourself and your siblings and work back methodically through parents and grandparents as far as you can go, not forgetting the uncles, aunts and cousins.

Ask as many relatives and family friends as you can for their recollections and reminiscences. Make a note of what each person says either: on paper, computer or by making a recording that can be written up later. Nobody ever recalls everything in one sitting, so be patient: several visits may be necessary if someone has a lot of information to share with you. One recollection tends to lead to another and you may find yourself bombarded with information, which, at the time, may not make much sense to you; therefore, keeping a record of some kind is the key to future research. Do not disregard any family stories, as you may later discover that there was some element of truth in them.

Encourage relatives to search for any family records and memorabilia they may have. Attics are a great place to search, given that they are often used to store papers, documents, photographs and newspaper cuttings that may well have been inherited and forgotten about. Showing such items to elderly relatives and family friends can often jog their memory, but bear in mind that keeping accurate records of what information was given in response, and where the records were originally found, is a very important part of being a good family historian. Compiling a list of questions to ask can also be a good starting point and can lead to much more information: ask who, where, when and why. However, be aware that 'skeletons in the cupboard' were often not talked about, so you may come across some reluctance to discuss certain aspects of your family's history.

The sort of ephemera you should look out for includes certificates: birth, marriage and death certificates are the most obvious ones, but keep an eye out for others that can assist you, such as baptismal, Sunday school and educational certificates. Newspaper cuttings are another wonderful source of information and very often hold connections with the family. Obituaries are very often cut out and

A selection of items that can be found whilst searching for family records. (Author's collection)

A collection of nineteenth-century memorial cards. (Author's collection)

kept, as are marriage photographs and newspaper records of other significant events relating to the family or the area where they lived.

Funeral leaflets and memorial cards are collections I have come across whilst doing my own research – and I have inherited collections from deceased relatives over the years. These do not always pertain directly to relatives, as they sometimes refer to people known to the family, but they can still hold enough information to search for a burial record, monumental inscription, death certificate and/or a newspaper obituary.

3

A collection of photographs that have been kept in the family. (Author's collection)

Family bibles can also be a valuable asset in your research if your family are lucky enough to have one that documents family members within its leaves. Other records to look for are family letters, diaries, deeds, rentals and any papers that can give you a bigger picture of the lives of family members at a given time. Photographs are the one item the majority of us have. However, very few have any details attached to them for identification purposes. If any friends or relatives can give you information about a photograph, make a note in pencil on the back for future reference.

Do not despair if you cannot find many details at the beginning. The minimum information you actually need to get started is your own date and place of birth.

Once you have gathered together some information, you need to get it organized into a family tree. This can be done on paper initially – and possibly on computer later on, by using a family tree software programme. Inevitably you will accumulate a mass of paper – copies of documents, photographs, newspaper cuttings, certificates, and so on. For ease of access, these should be arranged in files, either by individual or by family branch.

There are many family history software packages available on the market, which provide templates for organizing your family history research. The information you add is, in turn, used to create comprehensive reports and family tree charts – and you can include photographs, videos and online links with the majority of packages. It is therefore worth doing some research and checking out reviews, either online or in family history magazines, before buying.

You can get basic family tree packages from commercial sites; these are more than sufficient when you are beginning your research. These sites often provide this facility free of charge without a subscription; however, if you subscribe, they will also link your family history details to their databases and make suggestions of records that could fit your family tree. Many of these packages have apps that allow you to access your tree whenever and wherever you have an Internet connection, for example, when you are using a smartphone or a tablet.

Using online resources

Once you have done the preliminary work you will be ready to search further afield; you can begin either online, or by visiting/contacting a county archive office or the National Library of Wales. Online resources are constantly changing: new data sets are added to commercial and non-commercial sites on a regular basis. Before subscribing to one of the commercial packages, it is a good idea to make sure that they have data sets that are of use; you can do this by taking up the free trial that many of them offer (such trials are often available for a 14-day period). If you are researching in Wales, it is worth remembering that, at the time of writing, all Welsh archive offices and libraries have free access to the Ancestry website and to the parish registers that appear on the Findmypast website: so you can simply pop in and try both sites free of charge, with the advantage of having staff at hand to assist you. The majority of the main data sets on both sites cover Wales and include: census returns 1841–1911; General Register Office indexes to births, marriages and deaths; UK-based passenger lists; and the National Probate Calendar. Additionally, Welsh parish registers can be viewed, but are only available on Findmypast.

Two very useful portals for family history websites are Cyndi's List and Genuki, which both provide further information about – and links to – a variety of family history resources, not only for Wales but much further afield. They are a good starting point for those new to family history, as they offer some idea of what to expect in records, what type of information can be found and where to go for further information.

Another well-established free family history resource on the Web is Familysearch. This began its life many years ago, before the inception of the Internet, as the International Genealogical Index (IGI) and was available on microfiche, but is now available online. These records are gathered by The Church of Jesus Christ of Latter Day Saints (the Mormons or LDS) at their library in Salt Lake City, Utah, USA. They have branches of their Family History Centres around the world including eight in Wales (see Appendix 1 for details). The records include births and baptisms; marriages; deaths and burials; census returns; and probate. Certain of these records are linked to Findmypast, for which a subscription will be requested to view some of the information.

As online resources change constantly, I am not going into great detail here because the information will soon be out of date; however, no one these days will be able to do any family history research without at some point having to use the Web. Therefore, the sources I have referred to are a good starting point along with many others mentioned under specific subjects throughout this book.

Further reading

Blatchford, Robert, *The Family and Local History Handbook* (14 vols, Blatchford Publishing, York)

Durie, Bruce, *Welsh Genealogy* (The History Press, 2012)

Fowler, Simon, *Tracing Your Ancestors: A Guide for Family Historians* (Pen & Sword, 2011)

Foy, Karen, *Family History for Beginners* (The History Press, 2002)

Herber, Mark, *Ancestral Trails* (2nd edn, SOG, 2004)

Llwyd, Rheinallt and Owen, Huw, *Searching Community and Family History in Wales* (Carreg Gwalch, 2014)

Rowlands, John and Rowlands, Sheila, *Welsh Family History: A Guide to Research* (Gomer, Llandysul, 1993)

Rowlands, John and Rowlands, Sheila, *Second Stages in Researching Welsh Ancestry* (FFHS, 1999)

Websites

Ancestry **www.ancestry.co.uk**

Archives Wales **www.archiveswales.org.uk**

Association of Family History Societies of Wales **www.fhswales.org.uk**

Cyndislist **www.cyndislist.com/uk/wls/**

Findmypast **www.findmypast.co.uk**

Familysearch **www.familysearch.org/**

Genuki **www.genuki.org.uk/big/wal/**

Genealogy software **www.genealogy-software-review.topten reviews.com**

National Library of Wales **www.llgc.org.uk**

Chapter 2

THE WELSH

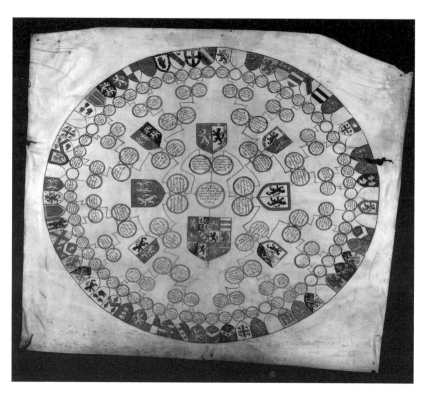

The pedigree of John Salisbury, compiled in 1627 by Jacob Chaloner. (NLW, Peniarth Ms 475G)

Pedigrees and Heraldry

It was once a legal necessity to know your Welsh pedigree as, according to the Welsh laws of Hywel Dda, you should be able to call upon your relative to the seventh or ninth generation. Proof of kinship was often called upon in cases of inheritance of land, settlement of disputes and other legal matters. There is very little evidence of Welsh heraldry before the mid-fourteenth century, much later than in England, and it did not gain in popularity until the fifteenth century. Owing to the lack of Welsh medieval rolls of arms, we are indebted to the bards who included genealogical information in their poetical works and, later, in their descriptions and illustrations of coats of arms.

Even after the Acts of Union in 1536 and 1543, when Wales came under English law and it was no longer necessary to know one's pedigree, the Welsh continued with the tradition of knowing their kinship: it was considered very important by them, as it is to this day. Edward VI first ordered a heraldic visitation to Wales in 1550, but it did not take place until soon after, when the English heralds first appointed Gwilym Hiraethog (d.1564) and, subsequently, Lewys Dwnn (d. *c.*1615) as deputy heralds for Wales. Both were traditionally trained bards and their writings have become an invaluable source in the history of Welsh heraldry. During this period, the majority of the works were written in Welsh, but later antiquarians wrote them in English. Pedigrees could also be in manuscript or tabular format. This is an English example from the works of Lewys Dwnn:

> Thomas Moiston Esquire, sonne and heire to William Moiston Esqe sonne and heire to Thomas Moiston Esqe sonne and heire to Richard ap Howel ap Ieuan vychan ap Ievan ap Addav ap Ierwerth ddy ap Ednyfed gam ap Ierwerth voel ap Ierwerth vychan ap yr hên Ierwerth ap Owain ap Bleddyn ap Tydyr ap Rys Sais ap Ednyfed ap Llwarch gam ap Llyddocka ap Tydyr Trevor Lord of Broomefield ap Ynyr ap Kadfarch. (Lewys Dwnn, Vol. II, p 307)

The earliest genealogical manuscript was written in the ninth century and others in the twelfth and thirteenth centuries. They contained details of the Welsh patriarchs, saints and prominent families. Very few early original manuscripts survive and many of the surviving manuscripts have been copied time and again, with later additions by genealogists and antiquarians. The bards of the fifteenth and sixteenth centuries not only copied older pedigrees, but also recorded many new ones. This was the period when it became popular for noble families in Wales to have pedigree rolls created for them with painted coats of arms, though many have no coats of arms. With the notable decline of the bards in the early seventeenth century, much of their good work was carried on by the antiquarians who collected their work. Many of these manuscripts form an important part of the early Welsh manuscript collection at the National Library of Wales. The library also has a comprehensive collection of Welsh pedigree rolls: others are held in county archives throughout Wales. These charts were produced in a range of shapes and sizes, and with much variation in detail. In *Welsh Pedigree Rolls*, Dr Michael Powell Siddons lists seven types of roll, one of the more unusual ones being a target pedigree, in which the coat of arms is in the centre and preceding generations are in concentric circles, working outwards. An example held at the National Library of Wales is the pedigree of John Salisbury, compiled in 1627 by Jacob Chaloner (NLW, Peniarth Ms 475).

There are inevitably errors within the manuscripts and pedigrees, as the originals were copied time and again: misinterpretations were made, persons of the same name were confused and these errors were passed on to the next copy. As with all sources used in tracing your family history, whenever possible the information gained should be used to direct you to other contemporary sources, so that you can verify what you have found out.

One notable distinction in Welsh heraldry was the retrospective attribution of a coat of arms to persons who had never lived or persons who were alive before the onset of heraldry. According Dr Siddons, 175 coats of arms were attributed to the knights of King Arthur's Round Table; additionally, the Trinity and many saints have also been attributed coats of arms.

The fact that a particular family bore a certain coat of arms does not mean that all families of the same name bore the same arms or were descended from the same family. Heraldic pedigree rolls were compiled from the late sixteenth century onwards. The English heralds carried out heraldic visitations for parts of Wales, recording coats of arms and some genealogical information. Many Welshmen recorded their pedigrees and arms in English counties where they lived. All these records are held at the College of Arms, London.

According to the College of Arms, the law relating to arms in England and Wales states that a person is entitled to use armorial bearings if one of three conditions are met:

- descent from a male line from a person to whom arms have been granted and recorded at College of Arms, London;
- proof of descent in the male line from a person who has been recognized as armigerous in a visitation by a member of the College; or
- obtained a grant of arms to himself.

Remember that a coat of arms does not belong to a surname, but to an individual, and only those who can meet one of the above conditions may bear a coat of arms. In order to find out if you have any entitlement use a coat of arms, the College of Arms should be your first port of call. You will need to provide a pedigree of your family that goes as far back as possible and is supported with documentary evidence. More information can be found on the website of the College of Arms.

I shall not go into the details of the composition of a coat of arms as there are many standard works that can be consulted for more information relating to heraldry in general, one being the work of Thomas Woodcock and J.M. Robinson. Furthermore, Welsh heraldry is covered in great detail by Dr Siddons.

The majority of important original manuscripts relating to Welsh pedigrees are held at the National Library of Wales, with the Peniarth manuscripts being the principal collection. However, there are some amongst collections in repositories throughout Wales, such as Bangor University, the Cardiff Central Library Manuscripts, the University of Swansea and the Carmarthen Archives. Further afield, there are manuscripts pertaining to Welsh pedigrees in the Bodleian Library, Oxford and the Harleian Collection at the British Library.

Some of the most important printed works relating to Welsh pedigrees are listed in the further reading section.

Language

There are probably two fundamental differences between researching Welsh and English family history. The first is the Welsh language and the second is the use of patronymics in Wales, as opposed to the use of fixed surnames in England. Anyone using Welsh records in their research will, at some point, come across information that is in the Welsh language. Therefore, a basic understanding of the language, using translation tools such as basic grammar, translation tables and dictionaries, can help overcome this obstacle.

Welsh is a Celtic language, along with Breton and Cornish, and is one of the most ancient living languages in Europe. Its origins can be traced back to the sixth century, when the earliest known Welsh literature was produced. The Books of Aneirin and Taliesin are thirteenth- and fourteenth-century manuscripts of Welsh literature attributed to poets who lived in the sixth century. These collections of poems and later manuscripts are very often the only sources for chronicling events and family relationships for many centuries. Later, the heralds of Wales also used Welsh to record pedigrees, Lewys Dwnn being a prime example. The translation of the Bible into Welsh, in 1588, to an extent standardized written Welsh for the people of Wales.

Official records were not written in Welsh: legal documents were written in Latin or English until 1733, and in English thereafter. This was also true for church records, but there is always an exception to the rule and very occasionally you may come across entries in parish registers or bishop's transcripts written in Welsh. Nonconformist records are probably more likely to be in Welsh, including baptism and burial registers, but usually the important information is easily identifiable: name, date, location. Original census schedules were available in Welsh from 1851; however, the enumerator had to translate any Welsh information into English so it could be entered in the enumerator's books. Subsequently, the census returns as we view them today are in English. The 1911 is the first census for which we are able to view the original schedules therefore many of these are in the Welsh language. Translation tables based on the information given on the 1911 census returns have been created and accessed on the Association of Family History Societies of Wales website. The information is a useful reference tool for Welsh translation across all sources of family and local history research and consists of:

- Forenames
- Relationship to head of household
- Birthplace
- Birthplace outside of Wales
- Other columns – age, infirmity, language, employment

One area where you will come across the use of the Welsh language is in the graveyard. Our ancestors probably spoke Welsh at some point in the past and many of them were bilingual, with Welsh as

Gravestones at Gwynfil Calvinistic Methodist Chapel, Llangeitho, Ceredigion. (Author's collection)

their first language. However, many early ancestors would have been monoglot Welsh-speakers and these ancestor's lives would have been commemorated on gravestones in Welsh. Gwen Awbrey's book is an excellent, comprehensive guide to use when wandering Welsh graveyards or researching transcriptions of monumental inscriptions: it contains several translation tables that include verses from the Bible and poetry that are often found on headstones.

There are also Welsh language newspapers and periodicals or the occasional piece in Welsh in the English language papers. These could well include important references and information relating to an ancestor and should not be dismissed because of a lack of knowledge of the Welsh language. Some basic Welsh can help decipher personal names, place names, dates, occupations and other invaluable information that can lead to other sources.

The Welsh alphabet uses twenty-eight letters, including eight digraphs (a pair of letters used as one letter), and does not include K, Q, V, X, Z:

A, B, C Ch, D, Dd, E, F, Ff, G, Ng, H, I, (J), L, Ll, M, N, O, P, Ph, R, Rh, S, T, Th, U, W, Y

Digraphs: Ch, Dd, Ff, Ng, Ll, Ph, Rh, Th

Vowels: A, E, I, O, U, W, Y

'J' has in recent years been accepted in the Welsh alphabet for words 'borrowed' from English such as 'jiwbilî' (jubilee), 'jwg' (jug) and words with the sound of 'j' such as 'garej' (garage).

When looking up a Welsh word beginning with a digraph in a dictionary, use the above alphabet as a guide for arrangement. Words commencing with 'll' will be found after those commencing with 'l', but remember to treat each digraph as a single letter: for example, note that 'ng' comes after 'g' and not after 'n'.

Mutation of the first letter of a word in Welsh grammar can make it difficult to find it in a dictionary, as the mutated form of a word will not be listed; in order to backtrack to the original form, the following table will be of use.

Original letter	Soft mutation	Nasal mutation	Aspirate mutation
B	F	M	
C	G	Ngh	Ch
D	Dd	N	
G	disappears	Ng	
Ll	L		
M	F		
P	B	Mh	Ph
Rh	R		
T	D	Nh	Th

Using Pontardawe as an example:

'Croeso i Bontardawe' (welcome to Pontardawe) – soft mutation P > B
'Mae'r t ym Mhontardawe' (the house is in Pontardawe) – nasal mutation P > Mh
'Caerdydd a Phontardawe' (Cardiff and Pontardawe) – aspirate mutation P > Ph

There are many useful websites available nowadays to help with translation: only a few have been noted here. Do not be put off by the use of Welsh, as it will only help to enrich your family history further. Staff at local repositories throughout Wales will be only too willing to help with or advise on any difficulties relating to the Welsh language.

Patronymics and Surnames
The patronymic naming system employed in Wales before the adoption of fixed surnames, as used in England, can be challenging if you are not aware of how it works. Each man's personal name was followed by 'ab' or 'ap' meaning 'son of', then the Christian name of his father, as in: 'Dafydd ap Gwilym' (David son of Gwilym). In the same way, a daughter's first name would be followed by 'ferch' or 'verch' often abbreviated to 'vch' or 'vz', then her father's

Christian name, as in: 'Margaret verch Robert' (Margaret daughter of Robert). A string of names indicates numerous generations: for example, Dafydd ap Gwilym ap Rhydderch ap Thomas, would be a string of four generations showing Dafydd as the son of Gwilym, grandson of Rhydderch and great-grandson of Thomas; Gwilym is therefore the son of Rhydderch and grandson of Thomas, and Rhydderch is the son of Thomas. After marriage, women tended to retain their maiden names during the period when patronymics

An example of the use of the patronymic naming system in burials, 1698, Llangelynnin parish, Caernarfonshire. (NLW, BTs Llangelynnin)

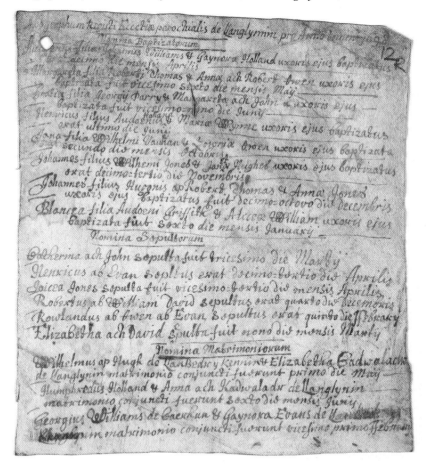

were used. A woman's maiden name would include the patronymic name of her father in many cases, as in: Margaret verch Robert ab Gruffydd (Margaret daughter of Robert son of Gruffydd).

It was not until the sixteenth century that Wales began to use fixed surnames, but it was a gradual process: the patronymic system had disappeared in the parishes on the English borders and in south Wales by the mid-eighteenth century, but lasted until the mid-nineteenth century in many Cardiganshire and Caernarfonshire parishes. When fixed surnames were gradually introduced they derived from personal names with the addition of an 's'. For example, Jones, Evans, Williams and Davies were derived from John, Evan, William and David. Others used the addition of a 'p' or 'b' derived from 'ap' or 'ab' at the beginning to produce surnames such as Bowen from 'ab Owen' and Powell from 'ab Howell'. The Christian names of fathers and grandfathers were adopted by the family as surnames, so Robert ap Richard became known as Robert Richard, often with the 's' added at the end to create 'Richards' and this would be the family surname forthwith. Sometimes the 'ab' or 'ap' was not used, as in the case of the baptism of:

> John son of David John Evan Morgan Mason by Ann his wife at Cilgerran, Pembrokeshire in 1775.

John was the son of David [son of] John [son of] Evan [son of] Morgan, and Mason was the occupation in this particular example, rather than a surname.

Variations in spelling also need to be taken into consideration when searching early records. Rees as we know it may well appear as Rice, Rhys, Reese, Reece or as a fixed surname such as Price, Pryce, Pryse, Preese, Preece. The simplest of names may have many variations and this should be borne in mind when difficulties are encountered in tracing ancestors.

It is generally thought that tracing a Welsh ancestor with a common surname is virtually impossible, but that is not the case. Once you have traced a family to a particular place, information from any name-rich source can be of great help in identifying the family within the community. Yes, there may be a few people with the same Christian and surname, but it is a process of elimination to determine the correct one by using the other information available: for example, a sibling may have a more uncommon name, so trace them backwards to the next generation.

Given that so few surnames were adopted in Wales, any additional information that can assist in the identification of individuals is a bonus. Names of houses can be very useful when you come across two people of the same name and approximate age, as was the case when I was recently researching the family of Thomas Williams in Merthyr Cynog. There were two individuals aged 50 years but, because I had the name of where they lived, I was able to determine that the correct one was Thomas Williams of Yskirfechan rather than the one living at Pentwyn.

It is very much a Welsh tradition to identify someone by where they live and this is still true today in rural Wales, for example: John, T. Draw; Morgan, Penlan; Edward, Lluest. Although they may not have been recorded in this way in official records, you might come across such references in personal documents and oral history.

The same can be said for the use of occupations in names; for example, oral tradition might refer to Twm y Gof (Thomas the blacksmith) or Jones y Saer (Jones the carpenter). Although occupations in their Welsh form might look unfamiliar to someone who is not a Welsh speaker, when these are listed in registers, census returns, other records or newspaper articles, they are usually in English (unless the records are in the Welsh language) and this can help to identify the correct individual – especially if where they lived is not recorded.

Place Names

Identifying Welsh place names correctly can also pose a problem for someone who is not familiar either with the geography of an area or with the Welsh language. Records sometimes use localized or shortened versions of a name along with the use of village, township and parish names, so access to a good gazetteer is recommended. For example, the village of Pontrhydfendigaid in Ceredigion is locally

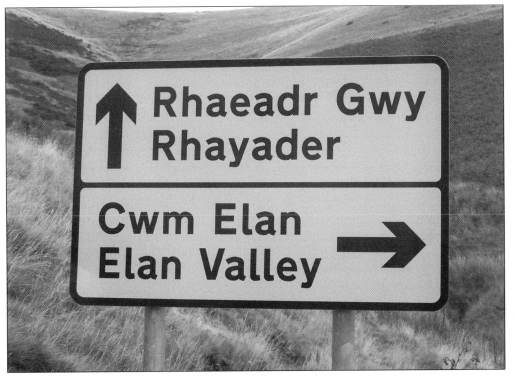

A road sign showing the use of both Welsh and English. (Author's collection)

known as Bont, but it is partly in the parish of Caron Uwch Clawdd and partly in Gwnnws Upper. Standard works that are usually referred to when researching Welsh family history are those of Melville Richards and Elwyn Davies; it can also be helpful to consult contemporary maps of the area in question alongside modern maps.

Another example is the name Bryngwyn, which could be the name of a house; a parish of Llan-arth, Monmouthshire; a township of Llanfihangel Aberbythych, Carmarthenshire; or the parish of Llanfihangel y Bryn-gwyn in Radnorshire. Therefore, using information from the records you are searching, with a map and gazetteer, will help identify the correct location – otherwise you may find yourself barking up the wrong tree!

19

'Llan' (usually meaning church) is a very popular first element of Welsh place names. There are nearly 600 parishes listed in *Cofrestri Plwyf Cymru/Parish Registers of Wales* with this first element, leading to second common elements such as 'Llanbedr', 'Llanbadarn', 'Llanfair' and 'Llanfihangel'. These in turn have other elements that help to determine the correct parish, which are often dedicated to a saint and include descriptive words of the location, as in: 'Llanbedr-ar-fynydd' (church of St Pedr on a mountain); 'Llanbadarn ' (large church of St Padarn); 'Llanfair juxta Harlech' (church of St Mary near Harlech); and 'Llanfihangel yn Nhywyn' (church of St Michael in Tywyn). Other frequently occurring first elements are 'aber' (estuary), as in Aberystwyth (estuary of the river Ystwyth), and 'eglwys' (church), as in 'Eglwysfach' (small church), amongst others.

There are many published books and articles relating to Welsh place names and these should be referred to for a more in-depth perspective on the meaning of names and how names evolved. There is no comprehensive list of all Welsh house names: however, Edwin C. Lewis' book is a good guide. Remember that there are English and Welsh forms for many places in Wales, as well as county and country names, some more familiar than others: Cardigan/Aberteifi, St Asaph/Llanelwy, Brecon/ Aberhonddu. You will more often than not find bilingual signs whilst travelling through Wales looking for your ancestors, so it is well worth making a note of them in the areas that are of interest to you. Again, the Association of Family History Societies of Wales website is a good starting point for translation tables relating to places.

Some very basic translation tables have been included in Appendix 2, for other tables refer to the works mentioned below.

Further reading

Awbrey, Gwen, *Tracing Family History in Wales: How to read the inscriptions on Welsh gravestones* (Carreg Gwalch, 2010)

Bartrum, Peter C., *Early Welsh Genealogical Tracts* (Cardiff, 1966)

Bartrum, Peter C., *Welsh Genealogies AD300–1400* (8 vols, Cardiff 1974)

Bartrum, Peter C., *Welsh Genealogies AD1400–1500* (18 vols, Aberystwyth, 1983)

Bradney, J. A., *A History of Monmouthshire* (6 vols, London, 1991–94)

Clark, G. T., *Limbus Patrum Morganiae et Glamorganiae: Being the Genealogies of the Older Families of the Lordships of Morgan and Glamorgan* (London, 1886)

Davies, Elwyn, *Rhestr o enwau lleoedd/A Gazetteer of Welsh Place-names* (UWP, Cardiff, 1967)

Dwnn, Lewys (ed. Meyrick, S. R.), *Heraldic Visitations of Wales* (2 vols, Llandovery, 1846)

Griffith, J. E., *Pedigrees of Anglesey and Carnarvonshire Families* (Wrexham, 1985)

Lewis, Edwin C., *A Pocketbook of Welsh House-names* (Dinefwr, Llandybie, 2004)

Lloyd, J. Y. W., *History of Powys Fadog* (6 vols, London, 1881–87)

Morgan, T. J. and Morgan, Prys, *Welsh Surnames* (UWP, Cardiff, 1985)

Richards, Melville, *Welsh Administrative and Territorial Units* (UWP, Cardiff, 1969)

Rowlands, John and Rowlands, Sheila, *The Surnames of Wales* (Gomer, Llandysul & NLW, 2014)

Siddons, Dr Michael Powell, *The Development in Welsh Heraldry* (4 vols, Aberystwyth, 1991–2006)

Siddons, Dr Michael Powell, *Welsh Pedigree Rolls* (Aberystwyth, 1996)

Green, F. (ed), *West Wales Historical Records* (14 vols, Carmarthen, 1912–1919)

Woodcock, Thomas and Robinson, J. M., *The Oxford Guide to Heraldry* (Oxford, 2001)

Wyn Owen, Hywel and Morgan, Richard, *Dictionary of the Place names of Wales* (Gomer, Llandysul, 2007)

Websites

A Dictionary of the Welsh language **www.welsh-dictionary.ac.uk/**

Archif Melville Richards Place-name Database **www.bangor.ac.uk/amr**

Association of Family History Societies of Wales **www.fhswales.org.uk**

College of Arms **www.college-of-arms.gov.uk**

Welsh Place-name Society

Chapter 3

ARCHIVES, LIBRARIES AND FAMILY HISTORY SOCIETIES

The National Library of Wales or one of the county archive offices will be your first port of call when you have gathered together your research. The National Library of Wales is situated in a large majestic building on Penglais Hill overlooking the seaside tourist town of

Screenshot of the National Library of Wales website. (NLW)

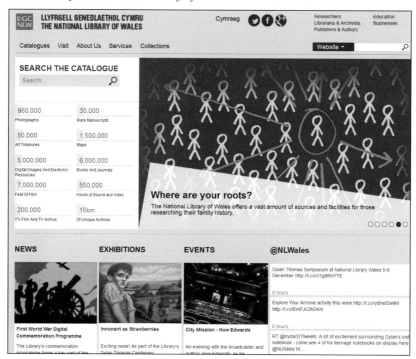

Aberystwyth, and Cardigan Bay. It is located in Aberystwyth in preference to Cardiff as Sir John Williams, physician to Queen Victoria and an avid book and manuscript collector, promised his collection to the library if it was established within the town. He was also later elected as the first president of the library. The Peniarth manuscripts he donated were amongst the foundation collections of the library and are of great importance to those searching family history as far back as the fifteenth and sixteenth centuries.

Frequent references to the collections held at the National Library of Wales will be made throughout this book, due to the variety of records held there. These records pertain to most aspects of family history research and relate to all areas of Wales. Hence, it is considered to be the main centre for researching family history in Wales. It is also the national legal deposit library of Wales, as it has the right to receive a copy of all books published in Great Britain. The library houses the following collections:

- 30,000 rare manuscripts
- 950,000 photographs
- 50,000 art works
- 1,500,000 maps
- 5,000,000 electronic resources and digital images
- 6,000,000 books and magazines
- 551,300 hours of sound, film and video
- 15km of unique archives

Once you have gathered your information and need to visit or contact the library, this can be done in a variety of ways:

- By completing the online enquiry form at: www.llgc.org.uk/enquiries
- By email, to: enquiry@llgc.org.uk
- By telephone: + 44 (0)1970 632 933
- By fax: +44 (0)1970 632 551
- By post, to: Enquiries Service, The National Library of Wales, Penglais, Aberystwyth, Ceredigion SY23 3BU
- By using the Quick Chat service, at:

www.llgc.org.uk/enquiries

As with most repositories these days, you will require a reader's ticket if you intend to visit in person. You can register online at www.llgc.org.uk/readersticket, where you can also check the necessary forms of identification that will be required to complete the process when you visit.

The library has a comprehensive catalogue http://cat.llgc.org.uk that can be searched using simple keywords, or combinations of keywords to narrow your search. This in turn can be filtered to search individual collections:

- Archives and manuscripts
- Archives Wales
- Books and journals
- Early books
- Film
- ITV Wales TV Archive
- Maps
- Marriage bonds
- Pictures
- Sound and video
- Wills

As well as other separate collections at http://www.llgc.org.uk/catalogue/ :

- Ballads
- Crime and punishment
- External e-resources
- Welsh journals
- Welsh biography
- Welsh newspapers

When visiting the National Library of Wales, it is well worth booking one of the information sessions available: www.llgc.org. uk/surgeries. These are sessions with a member of staff that last for half an hour and are designed to help you get to know the library, assist you with any brick walls you may have and advise you further on research.

Whilst the main aim of the National Library of Wales is to hold and conserve important historical records relating to the whole of Wales, such as personal, family, estate, society and business records, the county archive offices hold similar records for their own counties. If you are unsure which archive office holds the records you require, the Archives Wales website (http:// www.archiveswales.org.uk/) is the best place to start, as it shows basic catalogue descriptions of collections held all over Wales: not only at the county archive offices, but also at the National Library of Wales and university archives. It gives you tips not only for investigating family history, but also house history, local history and conducting academic research. Searches of the catalogue can be done:

- By subject
- By personal name
- By corporate name
- By place
- By repository
- By combined index search

Access to each office and facilities available will vary; therefore, you will need to check individual websites for details, or contact offices directly by telephone, especially if you intend to travel some distance to access information. Make sure that you check opening times and what form(s) of identification will be needed to obtain a reader's ticket. Find out what records they hold and how to gain access, as some record collections may have restrictions on them. Copying facilities are also important: find out if you are able to get photocopies or use your own camera to take photographs of relevant documents for your own personal use, as regulations are different in each office. Most of this information will be available on the offices' websites; a list of Welsh county archive offices can be found in Appendix 3.

It is well worth joining a family history society, as they hold a host of information in the indexes and transcriptions they produce, in the articles and contacts published within the covers of their journals, and in the wealth of knowledge and expertise possessed by long-standing members of the society. You could consider joining your local society to volunteer with their projects and to learn more about family history research and resources; you could also join a society for the area of your ancestors, in order to gain access to further information about the area they lived in.

Here is some information relating to the main Welsh family history societies that will give you a starting point. However, there will be many smaller groups within historical and local societies or one-name study groups that may also be relevant to your research. A great way to gain access to help and information is to attend one of the regional or national family history fairs: further information on these can be found on the relevant society websites.

Association of Family History Societies of Wales: www.fhswales.org.uk

All counties in Wales have their own family history society; therefore, in 1981 they grouped together to form the Association of Family History Societies of Wales (AFHSW). The aims of the association are to promote the study of family history and genealogy in Wales; to co-ordinate and support the activities of member societies in Wales; and to liaise with affiliate members and other appropriate bodies to represent the interests and needs of its member societies. All of the societies are also members of the Federation of Family History Societies, www.ffhs.org.uk/, an educational charity that supports, informs and advises its membership, which consists of family history societies and similar bodies across the world.

Cardiganshire Family History Society: www.cgnfhs.org.uk

The society was formed in 1995 to encourage those who have family connections within this historic county, wherever they may live, to study their genealogy and family history. Members meet on the fourth Tuesday of each month from September to November, January to June. The society publishes a journal three times a year in March, July and November. It has been actively contributing to the

National Burial Index Project (NBI) and has 163,000 entries relating to Cardiganshire on NBI3 (3rd edition of NBI). Publications include monumental inscriptions in booklet form and burial register entries on microfiche.

Clwyd Family History Society: www.clwydfhs.org.uk
The Clwyd Society was founded in 1980 and covers the north-east area of Wales: mainly Flintshire and Denbighshire. Its journal, *Hel Achau*, is published every quarter. Meetings are held in various places within the counties on the second Saturday afternoon of each month, except for August. Publications comprise a comprehensive collection of transcripts and indexes of parish registers, monumental inscriptions, nonconformist registers and directories from north Wales on CD-ROM or in booklet form. The website also has photographs of every parish church in north-east Wales.

Dyfed Family History Society www.dyfedfhs.org.uk
Dyfed covers the historic counties of Cardiganshire, Carmarthenshire and Pembrokeshire and was formed in 1982. The society has local branches in Llandovery, Haverfordwest, Cardigan, Llanelli and Carmarthen. The website should be checked for branch meetings as locations and times vary from branch to branch. The website hosts a collection of photographs of individuals, groups and buildings within the old county of Dyfed. The journal is published quarterly. Publications are on microfiche and CD-ROM and include parish registers, census returns, monumental inscriptions and vaccination records.

Glamorgan Family History Society: www.glamfhs.org.uk/
The society is central to all those with family history interests in the historic county of Glamorgan; it has branches in Aberdare and Cynon Valley, Bridgend, Merthyr Tydfil, Cardiff, Pontypridd and Rhondda, and Swansea. The society has a research centre at Aberkenfig, which is open every Wednesday between 10.30 am and 3.00 pm. It has a comprehensive collection of publications on microfiche and CD-ROM, from parish registers to registers of electors, rate assessments and more. The society also contributes to

the NBI project. Details of meetings can be found on the website.

Gwent Family History Society: www.gwentfhs.info
The Gwent society covers the historic county of Monmouthshire. Members receive a quarterly journal. There are five branches in: Blackwood, Chepstow and Wye Valley, Ebbw Vale and North Gwent, Newport, and Pontypool. Check the website for monthly meeting details as they vary from branch to branch. Publications are on microfiche or CD-ROM and again they have published an extensive list of records, such as parish registers, chapel records and census returns.

Gwynedd Family History Society: gwynnedfhs.org
The society was founded in 1980 to cater for those with Gwynedd ancestry and aims to help anyone in need of assistance with their research. *Gwreiddiau Gwynedd Roots* is the official publication of the society and is produced in April and November. It has a variety of publications for sale in microfiche or paper format. The society has six branches covering the north-west of Wales and the website should be checked for information relating to each branch.

Montgomeryshire Genealogical Society: www.montgomeryshiregs.org.uk/
The aim of the society is to encourage interest in family history within the historic county of Montgomeryshire and around its borders. Meetings are held in Newtown on the first Saturday of the month from September to November, and February to April. Numerous transcripts relating to registers and census returns are published on microfiche, CD-ROM or in booklet format. Their journal, *Record*, is issued three times a year.

Powys Family History Society: www.powysfhs.org.uk
The county of Powys comprises the historic counties of Breconshire, Radnorshire and Montgomeryshire. Each group holds its own meetings in Brecon, Llanddewi Ystradenny and Newtown respectively. The journal, *Cronicl*, is published three times a year.

Once again, the society has an extensive collection of publications of parish and nonconformist registers, census returns and memorial inscriptions available in booklet, microfiche or CD-ROM format. The society is also a contributor to the NBI project.

London Branch of the Welsh Family History Societies: www.rootsweb.ancestry.com/~wlslbfhs/

The society is a member of the Association of Family History Societies of Wales and an affiliated member of many of the county societies. It was formed to encourage and support those in and around London wishing to research their Welsh roots. They meet four times a year in central London and anyone with an interest in Welsh family history is very welcome to attend. One of their objectives is to index material that is of special interest to Welsh family historians and is located in London.

Chapter 4

CIVIL REGISTRATION

Civil registration of all births, marriages and deaths in England and Wales has been in force since 1 July 1837. Members of all religious denominations had to be registered as part of the government's attempt to monitor population trends. Before this central system was introduced, different denominations recorded vital events in various ways – or not at all in many cases – which not only made it difficult for the government to gather statistics on the population at the time, but has also made it hard for family historians, past and present, to trace their ancestors.

Both England and Wales were divided into registration districts, each one with its own superintendent registrar. These districts were further divided into local districts with their own local registrars and each registration district was given a volume number. From 1837 to 1851, two volumes covered the whole of Wales: Volume XXVI covered Breconshire, Carmarthenshire, Glamorganshire, Monmouthshire, Pembrokeshire, Radnorshire and the English border counties of Herefordshire and Shropshire; Volume XXVII covered Anglesey, Caernarfonshire, Cardiganshire, Denbighshire, Flintshire, Merionethshire and Montgomeryshire. A revision of the registration districts in 1852 saw the following coverage until 1946: Volume 11a covered Carmarthenshire, Glamorganshire, Monmouthshire and Pembrokeshire; Volume 11b covered Anglesey. Breconshire, Caernarfonshire, Cardiganshire, Denbighshire, Flintshire, Merionethshire, Montgomeryshire and Radnorshire.

Births and deaths had to be reported to the local registrar and this was usually done by a person connected to the event, such as a parent, in the case of a birth, or a person present at the time of a death. Marriages were reported by the clergyman or the local registrar who performed the ceremony. A record of all events was then forwarded by the local registrar to the superintendent registrar at the end of each quarter. In turn, the superintendent registrar would send copies of these certificates to the Registrar General at the General Register Office in London. From these certificates a central nationwide index was created at the General Register Office. Quarterly indexes were generated separately for births, marriages and deaths; the quarters were as follows:

- March – January, February and March
- June – April, May and June
- September – July, August and September
- December – October, November and December

Each quarterly index volume is arranged alphabetically by surname and gives forename, registration district, volume number and page number; this continues until 1984, from which time only one annual index was compiled.

Before you are able to obtain any certificates, a search will have to be made of the General Register Office (GRO) index. The index will provide the information required to order a copy of a certificate. The indexes from 1837 to 1984 are available to search on microfiche at the National Library of Wales and at many county archive offices and public libraries throughout Wales. However, the complete index from 1837 to 2006 is also available digitally and can be viewed on various commercial websites; some sites are available to access free of charge at the National Library of Wales, county archive offices and public libraries. Bilingual certificates have been available since 1969.

FreeBMD is an ongoing project aiming to transcribe the GRO indexes of births, marriages and deaths for England and Wales and to provide free Internet access to the transcribed records. The transcribing is done by volunteers and contains index information for the period covering 1837 to the end of 1983. Although the index is far from complete, it is well worth searching.

Births
A rough idea of when someone was born is usually needed before searching the indexes, especially if the name is a common one. This

information can usually be estimated from other sources such as census returns and marriage certificates. Parents have up to six weeks to register a birth, so you will need to bear this in mind when searching the index because they were compiled from dates of registration and not dates of birth. Therefore, a baby born on 25 March may well have been registered in April and would then appear in the June quarter for that year and not in the March quarter, as you might expect.

The information found in the birth index is surname, forename (second names were shown by initial from 1911 to 1965), registration district, volume and page number; from September 1911, the maiden name of mother is also included.

You may come across a short birth certificate amongst family papers, this is an extract of the full birth certificate and only shows the name and surname, date of birth, place of birth and sex of the child; applying for a full certificate may give you some new information.

The birth certificate gives the following details:

• When and where the baby was born (the date and place of birth). Early records may only give the name of the village or street, but later records will give a full address. The address was not always where the parents were living because the birth may have occurred in a workhouse, hospital, nursing home or the home of a relative. If there is a time recorded on the certificate, this may indicate that the baby was one of a multiple birth. This can be checked by searching the index for other entries of the same surname within the same registration district and with the same GRO reference number.
• Name, if any. All given names of the baby should appear; if a name had not been decided, 'male' or 'female' would be entered. It was possible to add or change a name for up to twelve months after registration. If you cannot find an entry under the known name it is worth checking the 'male' and 'female' entries at the end of the surname index for the registration district in question.

• Name and surname of father. This section should show the first name and surname of the father; if it is blank, this usually indicates that the parents were not married and that the child was illegitimate. Before 1875, the mother could give any name as that of the father; however, after this date the father had to accompany her to the register office if they were not married, in order for his name to be included on the certificate. After 1969, the father's place of birth was also included.

• Name, surname and maiden surname of mother. This section will show the first name of the mother and any other surnames she has previously been known by: thus providing her maiden name and indicating any previous marriages. After 1969, the mother's place of birth is also included.

• Occupation of father. This can be useful to know, especially when you are searching for common names and need to differentiate between fathers. However, bear in mind that occupations can change between certificates and census returns. After 1984, the mother's occupation is also recorded.

• Signature, description and residence of informant. The name that appears here is usually one of the parents; however, if it is a different name, their relationship to the baby and their address should also be included. If the address is the same as where the child was born it may indicate that the child was delivered at home.

• When registered. It was compulsory to register a birth within forty-two days, otherwise a fee was payable. This date indicates when the informant went to the register office to register the birth (rather than the exact date of the birth) and it is this date that is used to compile the GRO index; therefore, as mentioned previously, the birth may have been registered in the quarter after the child was born.

• Signature of registrar. This is the name of the local registrar who registered the birth.

• Name entered after registration. This is usually crossed through unless a name was added or changed during the twelve months after birth, in which case any changes would be entered in this column. If a child was later adopted, the date of adoption would be entered in this column, but the child's new name would not be given for protection reasons.

The birth certificate of Thomas William, Eglwysilan, Glamorganshire, 1857. (NLW, Bute D161/7)

Stillbirths

Records of stillbirths in England and Wales have only been kept since 1 July 1927 and special permission is required before any information from these records is given out by the Registrar General. Prior to 1927, stillbirths were recorded only as deaths, but may be entered as stillbirths in parish burial registers. No official records pertaining to stillbirths are held separately for Wales: all are held by the Registrar General.

Adoptions

The Adopted Children Register was not introduced until 1927; it holds records of registered adoptions that were authorized by court orders. The index is available at The National Archives (TNA) and is searchable by the child's adoptive name. Full adoption certificates will only be supplied to the adoptive person and will not be issued to the public. Prior to 1927, no formal adoptions were recorded: many were done privately or through charitable organizations. For adoptions that took place before 1975, counselling is necessary before an original birth certificate can be issued. This is not always the case for adoptions after 1975. No official records or indexes for adoption are held separately for Wales.

Marriages

Marriage dates can be deduced by using other information if the date is not known. If the date of birth of the eldest child is known and the parents were married at this time, a search through every quarter from that date backwards is suggested. However, details from the 1911 census can also be of assistance, as these include a record of how long a couple had been married. Therefore, periods to be searched can be narrowed by using information relating to children and details found on census returns. Furthermore, the advent of online searching facilities has made the task of finding a marriage easier, unless common names are being sought.

In the GRO index, the names of the bride and groom will be listed separately under their respective names and arranged alphabetically by surname. The record will also give the registration district, along with the volume and page number. From the March quarter of 1912, the surname of the other party is shown in the index; this is a great asset for correctly tracing marriages for which both surnames are known.

A marriage certificate gives the following information:

• The place of marriage. The name of the church, chapel or register office; the parish and county where the ceremony took place appears along the top of the certificate.
• When married. The full date on which the marriage ceremony took place.
• Name and surname. The full names of the bride and groom. Look out for the bride's surname being different from that shown for her father, as it may indicate that this is a second

or subsequent marriage, or that she was born out of wedlock.

• Age. This will frequently show as 'of full age', indicating that the party was over the age of 21. If shown as 'minor' the party would be under the age of 21.

• Condition. Whether a bachelor or spinster, widower or widow and, after 1858, whether either party was divorced.

• Rank or profession. The occupation of the groom was usually given, but that of the bride was rarely stated; this did not always mean that she did not work and a search of census returns may give other information as to her occupation.

• Residence at the time of marriage. A couple would traditionally marry in the bride's parish and, if so, both had to live in the parish for the four weeks preceding the marriage; therefore, addresses shown on a certificate may not always be the permanent place of residence.

• Father's name and surname. This was always the name of the birth or adoptive father; the mother's name was never entered. Sometimes no name will appear, which suggests that the bride or groom was an illegitimate child, or that the party in question never knew the name of their father. However, if the father had died prior to the ceremony, sometimes the name would be given, followed by 'deceased', or the father's name would be omitted and only 'deceased' recorded.

• Rank or profession of father. The father's occupation; 'deceased' may appear here if he had died.

• Whether the marriage was by licence or after banns. A licence had to be paid for, but was a quicker and more private way to get married, especially if the wedding was to take place in the register office or in a parish other than the couple's home parish. All marriages by banns had to take place in the parish church, where the banns would be read for the three successive Sundays prior to the marriage. Further information relating to marriage banns or licences can be found in Chapter 6.

• The signatures of the bride and groom. One or both parties would sign their name or mark the paper with an 'X'; the latter often suggests that the signee was illiterate.

• The signatures of at least two witnesses: these may be relatives, friends or not even known to the couple. However, if the witnesses had surnames in common with either the bride or groom, it may be worth checking to see if there are any family connections. Again if the signee marked 'X', they may have been illiterate.

The marriage certificate of David Lloyd George and Margaret Owen, Pencaenewydd Chapel, Caernarfonshire. (NLW, Ms 20477C)

Deaths

Death certificates are not always necessary; however, they can contain information that was previously unknown. The cause of death could have been unusual, or due to an accident, which would therefore open other avenues of research such as coroners' records or newspaper reports. Death certificates can also reveal the date and place of birth of the deceased after 1969.

The GRO index lists the deceased alphabetically by surname; the age at death is included between 1866 and 1969; after 1969, the date of birth, registration district, and volume and page number are shown.

A death certificate gives the following information:

• When and where the individual died. This will be the place and date of death. The address given will not necessarily be where they were living, unless they died at home. They may have died at a relative's house, whilst visiting others, at the workhouse, in hospital or by tragic accident. This information may lead you to other sources such as workhouse, hospital or coroners' records and newspaper reports.

• Full name. This may be the name the deceased was known by at time of death and not necessarily their name at birth. From 1969, the maiden name of a married woman was also shown.

• Sex. Whether the deceased was male or female.

• Age at death. Prior to 1 April 1969, the informant gave the age of the deceased to the best of their knowledge, which left room for inaccuracy. From 1 April 1969 onwards, the date and place of birth were recorded. Children's ages tend to be accurate as the death had to be registered by one of the parents.

• Occupation of the deceased. However, other information is often included such as details of the father, if the death was of a child; in the case of a woman it may show who she was 'wife of' or 'widow of'.

• Cause of death. After 1874, it was compulsory for a death to be certified by a doctor before a death certificate could be issued. Websites, such as those listed in the further reading section, can help with the diagnosis of causes of death shown on death certificates.

• Signature, description and residence of informant. This would usually be a person present at the death, such as a relative, neighbour or doctor. If there was an inquest into the death, the coroner's name would appear and a search for more information could be made for the coroner's report in the local newspaper or local record office.

• When registered. The death had to be registered within five days unless there was a post-mortem or inquest.

• Signature of registrar. The signature of the local registrar who registered the death.

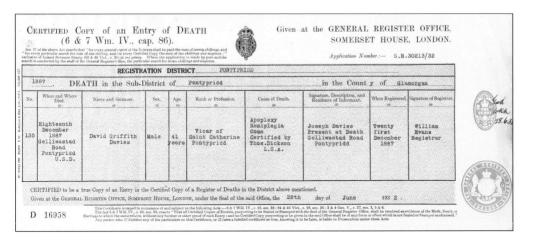

The death certificate of David Griffith Davies, Pontypridd, 1887. (NLW, Shadrach and Lewis Pryce Papers 71)

You can order copies of any certificate online, by telephone or by post through the General Register Office:

- Online: www.direct.gov.uk/gro
- By telephone: 0845 603 7788 Mon–Fri 8 am–8 pm, or Sat 9 am–4 pm
- By post: A completed GRO application form should be returned to General Register Office, PO Box 2, Southport, Merseyside, PR8 2JD

Alternatively, you can apply directly to the local register office where the certificate is housed. Further information on which office covers which area can be found at: http://www.ukbmd. org.uk/genuki/reg/

The website gives the following for each district:

- Name of the district.
- Registration county – many districts crossed county boundaries, but were classed wholly in one registration county for registration and census purposes.
- Date of creation.

• Date of abolition (if before 1974).
• Names of the sub-districts.
• The General Register Office (GRO) volume numbers used for the district in the national indexes of births, marriages and deaths.
• A list of the civil parishes or townships included within its boundaries. These often differ from the ancient parishes used until the early nineteenth century.
• The name(s) of the district(s) which currently hold(s) the records. If two or more offices are listed, the one which holds the most records is named first, and the one with the least is given last. A list of current register offices covering Wales can be found in Appendix 3.

There is also an alphabetical list of districts and an index of place names for the whole of England and Wales.

If you are searching for a certificate registered in north Wales, you may wish to search the online database of north Wales BMD. Clwyd and Gwynedd Family History Societies, along with Montgomeryshire Genealogical Society are collaborating with the local register offices to make the indexes to births, marriages and deaths available online, free of charge. Although the indexes are not yet complete for all years and districts, it is hoped that the database will eventually cover all registrations for north Wales from 1837 to 1950.

Other indexes held by the General Register Office that are often overlooked, or not known about, are the various records of vital events that occurred abroad (see table below). These will of course include numerous Welsh people and should not be forgotten if family had military or overseas connections. Microfiche indexes to these are held at the National Library of Wales and some of the indexes can also be found online on commercial websites.

ABROAD		
Regimental records	Records of births/baptisms, marriages and some deaths relating to British Army regiments	1761–1924
Chaplains' returns	Army chaplains' records of baptisms, marriages and deaths	1809–80
Ionian Islands	Births, marriages and deaths records of the British garrison on Corfu	1818–64
Marine records	Births and deaths at sea	1837– present date
Consular records	Births, marriages and deaths of British subjects registered at British consulates	1849–1912 months prior to present date
Army records	Births, marriages and deaths of members of the British Army or their families	1881–1965
War deaths	Deaths of serving personnel during the Boer War, First World War, Second World War	1899–1902 1914–21 1939–48
Aircraft records	Births and deaths on board British registered aircraft	1947– present date
High commission records	Births and deaths of British subjects registered at British high commissions	1949– present date

Further reading

Annal, David and Collins, Audrey, *Birth, Marriage and Death Records* (Pen & Sword, 2012)

Watts, Christopher T. and Watts, Michael J., *Tracing Births, Deaths and Marriages at Sea* (SOG, 2004)

Websites

FreeBMD **www.freebmd.org.uk**

General Register Office **www.gov.uk/general-register-office**

Medical terms and causes of death **www.archaicmedicalterms.com/**

North Wales BMD **www.northwalesbmd.org**

UKBMD **www.ukbmd.org.uk/**

Chapter 5

CENSUS RECORDS

The British government has taken a census of the population of England and Wales every ten years since 1801, but no names were given in the official returns of 1801 to 1831, only a figure for the number of people, the number of houses inhabited and the number uninhabited. As always, there are exceptions: sometimes records were made of the inhabitants' names and Appendix 4 lists those that survive for Welsh census returns between 1801 and 1831.

From 1841, once the census returns were completed and sent to the government, the originals were destroyed; but again, there are exceptions, such as the 1841 enumerator's book for Bromfield hundred, Wrexham, which was found in a second-hand bookshop in the 1970s. The book is now held at the Denbighshire Archives and it has now been transcribed and indexed by the Clwyd Family History Society.

The census was not taken in 1941, due to the outbreak of the Second World War, but it is hoped that the information from the national registration scheme that took place at the time, and data from national identity cards, will help plug the gap for future researchers of this period. Additionally, the census returns for 1931 were completely destroyed by a fire at the stores in Hayes, Middlesex on 19 December 1941, so these will not be available for consultation in the future.

Using the census to help your research can certainly open new doors. The age given on a census can help to trace a birth or baptism and information from more than one census can help discover an approximate date for a marriage, or when someone died. The details that can be obtained from census information over the years show how much change has occurred in the way our ancestors lived, in terms of work; reaching milestone ages; population; the number of people within families; depopulation in rural areas; and language. Excepting 1841, as less detail was asked for, a wealth of information can be gleaned from the forms that contain the names of those who were in a particular house on a particular Sunday night: their ages, how they were related, whether they were married or not, their occupations and their places of birth.

To ensure privacy, the information from each census has been closed to public access for 100 years. It was believed that all who were named would have died within 100 years: in 1891, for example, only five people in Wales were recorded as being over 100 years of age. In 1841, the census for England and Wales became the responsibility of the superintendent registrar, who was employed by the General Register Office; new census districts were also created at this time. Names were included for the first time on the 1841 census and from that time onwards the census records have listed all those living or staying in every house on census night, which has always been a Sunday night. It was believed a Sunday night was when most people would be at home.

1841 was also the year that enumerators were paid for the first time. The men were responsible for visiting about 250 houses in their district. They would start by distributing forms, which were designed to be completed by the family, and then they would collect them, in the hope that they had been completed correctly. In truth, the enumerators often had to complete the forms on behalf of householders because many were illiterate and they had to deal with those that did not co-operate.

The enumerators copied the information from the forms into enumerators' books, which are the basis of the images seen today; the original forms were subsequently destroyed. The books were arranged according to registration district, sub-district and parish. The front page of each book would give the enumerator the opportunity to describe their journey as they collected the forms, which can be useful when trying to locate a particular building within the parish, especially in rural settings. Being a census enumerator was not always an easy task. It was a more pleasurable and friendly job in the countryside as usually the enumerator was

1841 Census for Yskirfechan township, Merthyr Cynog parish, Breconshire, which shows the ages of the householders rounded down to the nearest 5 years. (TNA, HO 107/1368/13 p.6) local and knew everyone in his district. Each enumerator was required to be able to read, write and perform basic arithmetic. They had to be aged between 18 and 65 – and they needed to be fit, as there was a lot of walking involved. Enumerators in the larger towns were not always warmly welcomed because they were often mistaken for the 'rent man' or another official. They also had problems when it came to collecting the forms and, of course, getting the necessary information from respondents. In 1891, 35,000 enumerators were required throughout England and Wales and as there was a shortage of men to fill all the posts, it was decided that female enumerators would be used for the first time.

What applies to census returns for England also applies to Wales, except for a few special features. The household schedule distributed by the enumerator to each house was available in Welsh from 1841; however, if a Welsh schedule was completed, the enumerator had to translate the information, as the enumerators' books had to be completed in English. The result of this was that house and place names were translated to English even though they would normally have been known by a Welsh name: for example, 'The Tanhouse' would be have been known locally as 'Tanws'. Local accents and local dialects also need to be taken into consideration because the enumerators recorded what they heard – or what they thought they heard – which gave plenty of scope for names and place names to be recorded incorrectly.

From 1871 onwards, the enumerators indicated a Welsh household by placing a 'W' in the first column of the schedule. Many researchers may be interested in knowing whether the family were Welsh speakers or not, but the absence of a 'W' does not necessarily indicate that the household were not able to speak Welsh. From 1891, a question was included on the ability to speak Welsh. All schedules distributed in Wales asked respondents to indicate if they were able to speak Welsh, English or both; although from 1901, children under the age of 3 were not included in this question. Before 1891, no one had gathered any definite information about the number of Welsh speakers. Even in 1891, the correct statistics were not available because along the Flintshire and Monmouthshire borders, forms for England were distributed, rather than those for Wales that contained the language question. In 1891, the official figure for Welsh speakers was 60 per cent, a figure that has been in decline ever since: it had dwindled to 19 per cent in 2011.

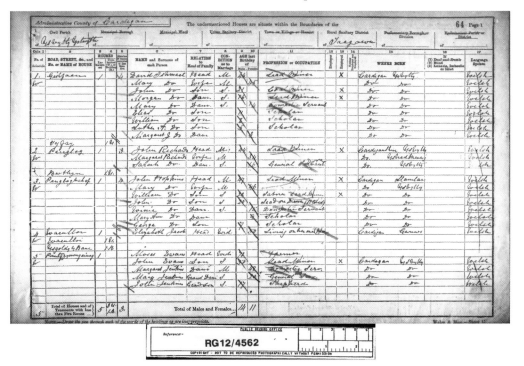

1891 census for the parish of Ysbytty Ystwyth, Cardiganshire. The form shows a 'W' in the first column, which indicates that the original household schedules were completed in Welsh and that the occupants all appeared to be monoglot Welsh-speakers. (TNA, RG12/4562/64 p.1)

Information columns for the 1841 census returns:

- Place – this is not always precise, it is often the name of a hamlet, township, or street.
- Houses – these were subdivided into inhabited buildings and uninhabited buildings.

47

• Name of each person who abode therein the preceding night – only one forename was recorded, even if a person had more than one. No relationship to the head of household was recorded, which means that relationships should not be assumed until other sources have been consulted and information verified.

• Age and sex, subdivided into male and female – the age was not precise except for those under the age of 15; for those over the age of 15 it was rounded down to the nearest five: for example, 23 years would appear as 20 and 48 years as 45. The ages given were often incorrect because knowing your age was not important at the time and, furthermore, there were numerous reasons why a respondent might state the wrong age.

• Profession, trade employment or of independent means.

• Where born and whether born in same county – 'Y' for Yes; 'N' for No.

• Where born and whether born in Scotland ('S'); Ireland ('I'); or foreign parts ('F').

Information columns for the 1851–1901 census returns:

• No. of householders schedule: each house was numbered on the schedule.

• Name of Street, Place or Road, and Name or No of House: houses were better recorded from 1851 onwards; however, houses were not always numbered within streets until much later censuses; numbering may not always follow and re-numbering between censuses was very common in developing towns.

• Name and Surname of each Person who abode in the house on the Night of the 30th March 1851: from 1861 to 1891 for second and subsequent names initials were to be used. From 1901 full names were given.

• Relation to Head of Family: included from 1851 onwards, of great assistance to researchers; however, beware of incorrect relationships, especially when there was more than one family living in the same household.

• Condition as to marriage: whether married, unmarried/single, widow or widowed.

• Age: subdivided into Male and Female from 1851 was more precise, however, there are occasions when ages were still given incorrectly.

• Rank, Profession or Occupation: more detailed occupations were included from 1851 onwards.

• Where born: more detail included from 1851, usually county and parish.

• Whether Blind, or Deaf and Dumb: from 1871 imbecile or idiot and lunatic were added, this subsequently changed in 1891 to imbecile, idiot or lunatic and in 1901 to lunatic and imbecile, feeble-minded.

• Language spoken: this was introduced as an extra column in Wales from 1891 onwards, recording ability to speak Welsh, English or both. Those under the age of 3 were not to be included from 1901.

It is worth pointing out at this stage that there are many schedules that are missing or incomplete, especially from the 1861 census. A list of the Welsh schedules can be found in Appendix 5.

The 1911 census is slightly different to previous censuses, as the original forms filled in by each head of household have been digitized, along with the enumerators' summary books, whereas only the enumerators' summary books were available for previous censuses. Therefore, for the first time we are able to see the handwriting of our ancestors. In Wales, forms were also provided in Welsh and many were completed in Welsh. The 1911 census is also known as the 'fertility census': the falling birth rate, decrease in population and the state of the nation's health prompted the government to include a question in the 1911 census on 'fertility in marriage'. The wife was asked how many years she had been in her present marriage; how many children had been born into the marriage; and how many of the children were still alive. Therefore, a marriage date can be found fairly easily from this information, as in the case of George William and Minnie Ada Bishop of Swansea, who recorded that they had been married for '2 years and 4 months' precisely. Occasionally this information was also completed for the husband, widower or widow and, although it would have been crossed out later, it can still be of use to family historians.

Previously unknown children who may have died in infancy, or were not known of before the census, as well as children who were away from home at the time of the census, could all be identified from this information. For example, in the case of David and Amelia Rees, of Swansea, who had been married for four years: they had two children and both were still living, but no children are listed in the household. In previous returns one might have thought that they had not had any children but, due to the additional information from the 1911 census, a search can be made for the children. Previous marriages may also be detected as a result of the ages of children being greater than the years in the present marriage, although this may also indicate illegitimate children.

Information columns for the 1911 census:

- Name and surname.
- Relationship to head of family.
- Age (last birthday) and sex – subdivided into ages of males and ages of females.
- Particulars as to marriage – for all persons aged 15 years and upwards, it was noted whether they were single, married, widower or widow.
- State of each married woman – subdivided into:
  - Completed years the present marriage had lasted
- Children born alive into present marriage – subdivided into:
  - Total children born alive
  - Children still living
  - Children who have died
- Profession or occupation of persons aged 10 years and upwards – subdivided into:
  - Personal occupation
  - Industry or service with which worker is connected
  - Whether employer, work or working on own account
  - Whether working at home

- Birthplace of every person – this included county, and town or parish.
- Nationality of every person born in a foreign country.
- Infirmity – totally deaf or deaf and dumb; totally blind; lunatic; imbecile or feeble-minded.
- Language spoken – English, Welsh, both; no entry was included for children under the age of 3.
- Number of rooms in the dwelling.

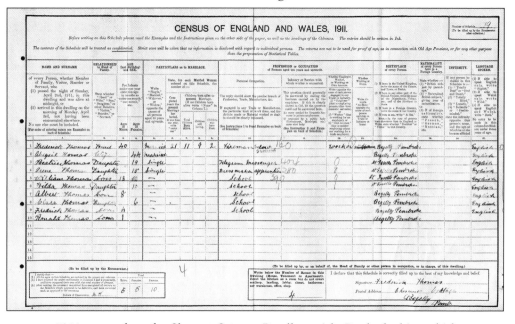

1911 census form for Chesnut Cottage, Begelly parish, Pembrokeshire, which shows information that relates to the length of the marriage and details of the children. This example demonstrates that this information was often recorded under the husband rather than the wife. (TNA)

Tracing Welsh ancestors can sometimes be difficult when using the 1911 census, due to the fact that the schedules were completed in Welsh. Further information relating to available translation tables aimed at the 1911 census can be found in Chapter 2.

When checking census returns, it is advisable to make a record of the full reference number of each page that is of interest to you;

each census has been given a different class number, followed by the enumeration district number, folio and page number. The class number and date of each census is as follows:

- HO107   1841 6 June
- HO107   1851 30 March
- RG9   1861 7 April
- RG10   1871 2 April
- RG11   1881 3 April
- RG12   1891 5 April
- RG13   1901 31 March
- RG14   1911 2 April

Be wary of any information found on census returns, there may well be discrepancies between different census years, so always try to verify data by checking with other sources. Ages in particular can vary; people often did not know or could not remember their age, or gave an incorrect age for other reasons. It is worth being aware of the fact that in the 1841 census ages were sometimes recorded as given by the householders, rather than rounded down to the nearest 5 years; nevertheless, the ages given on later censuses tended to be more accurate. Follow your family through all the censuses to 1911 so that a full picture can emerge; this will allow you to view and analyse information about several generations of one branch of your family simultaneously. You can save time by printing the relevant census pages from the website or by saving them to your computer; alternatively, you can transcribe the information in full, making a note of the full reference number for future use. Gazetteers can be useful in determining the locations of unfamiliar place names and what parishes they were part of.

Another census that is rarely mentioned in family history research is the 1851 religious census. This has only taken place once and it was undertaken because the government wished to gain a better picture of religious provision in England and Wales. This census was taken on Sunday 30 March 1851, the same night as the population census.

The aim of the 1851 religious census was to gather statistical evidence of those attending services and was completely voluntary. Each church, chapel and religious establishment received a schedule to be completed. Transcripts of the returns for Wales have been published by Ieuan Gwynedd Jones.

As Wales was a very nonconformist country at the time, information relating to religious churches and chapels in a particular area can be of assistance when determining where our ancestors may have worshipped, if not in the parish church. It also gives an insight into religious traditions in Wales and shows the importance of schools held in churches and chapels, such as Sunday schools and day schools, to the education of our ancestors. The following is an example of information given by the religious census:

Llansantffraid Parish, Aberayron (District), Cardiganshire
Nebo. Independent.
Erected: 1809; rebuilt 1833
Space: free; other 150; standing 100
Present: morn[ing] 170; aft[ernoon] 125 scholars; even[ing] 120 (see below)
Average: church members, 96
Remarks: chiefly a place of worship, but it has been occasionally employed as a day school. The Sunday School is always held therein. The chapel will hold about 400 persons. Evening: either a sermon or a prayer meeting at which on an average, 120 persons attend.
In this part, grown up persons and regular members of the churches as well as very young children regularly attend Sunday Schools.
Thomas Jones, Independent Minister.

Many family history societies and individuals have transcribed and indexed census returns over the years; therefore, it is well worth contacting societies, county archive offices or the National Library of Wales to see what is available, if you do not wish to pay to view the information. Bear in mind that any information found should be verified by comparing it with images of the original pages.

Further reading
Christian, Peter and Annal, David, *Census: The Expert Guide* (The
National Archives, 2008)
Hanson, John, (FSG) *How to Get the Best from the 1911 Census*
(SOG, 2009)
Higgs, Edward, *Making Sense of the Census Revisited: Census Records
for England and Wales, 1801–1901 – a Handbook for Historical
Researchers* (Institute of Historical Research, 2005)
Gibson, Jeremy and Medlycott, Mervyn, *Local Census Listings
1522–1930: Holdings in the British Isles* (3rd edn, FFHS, 1997)
Gwynedd Jones, Ieuan and Williams, David, *The Religious Census of
1851: A Calendar of the Returns Relating to Wales, Volume 1 South
Wales; Volume 2 North Wales* (University of Wales Press, 1976)
Raymond, Stuart A., *Census 1801–1911: A Guide for the Internet Era*
(The Family History Partnership, 2009)

Websites
Ancestry **www.ancestry.co.uk**
Association of Family History Societies of Wales
www.fhswales.org.uk
Findmypast **www.findmypast.co.uk**
Freecen **www.freecen.org.uk**
Genesreunited **www.genesreunited.co.uk**
UK Census Online **www.ukcensusonline.com**
The Genealogist **www.thegenealogist.co.uk**
The National Archives, Census guide
**www.nationalarchives.gov.uk/records/research-guides/
census-returns.htm**

Chapter 6

BAPTISMS, MARRIAGES AND BURIALS

The order for keeping parish registers – a record of all baptisms, weddings and burials in each parish throughout England and Wales – was first given by Thomas Cromwell, Henry VIII's chief minister, in 1538. However, these early registers held very little detail because all that was required was a record of the day and year of the event, along with the Christian name and father's name for baptisms, the name of the deceased for burials and the names of both parties for marriages. Over the following two centuries or so, little change occurred with regard to the recording of our ancestors' vital events. It was also required that these registers were kept in a secure coffer with two locks, which was often referred to as the 'parish chest'.

Towards the end of the sixteenth century, it became evident that the registers, which were written on loose leaves of paper, were in poor condition. In 1597, an order was made to all ministers to purchase parchment registers and to copy all previous entries, from 1538 onwards, into these new registers. Many only copied entries from the commencement of the reign of Elizabeth I in 1558, which is the reason that this date is often a starting point for numerous registers in England. However, only one parish in Wales – Gwaunysgor in Flintshire – has any records going back to 1538. Registers dating from the sixteenth century are fairly common in England. But in Wales, only four parishes have records that pre-date 1550; only one in six Welsh parishes have registers that date from before 1660; and only one in three parishes have records from before 1700. Several factors have been attributed to the poor survival rate of parish registers in Wales, compared to those in England, which include: ineffective organization, poverty, remote churches, and sparse population.

Also, as part of the 1597 order, the incumbent of each parish was required to send copies of all entries from the preceding year to the bishop of their diocese. These are known as bishops' transcripts. In England, bishops' transcripts go back to 1603; however, in Wales there are none earlier than 1661. The dioceses of St Asaph and Bangor have transcripts dating 1661–62, but for St Asaph these mostly cover the years between 1670 and 1850 and for Bangor the best coverage is for the years between 1675 and 1880. The transcripts for Llandaff diocese do not commence until 1725, whilst for St David's diocese, the Carmarthenshire and Gower archdeaconries have transcripts commencing from 1671; in the archdeaconry of Brecon, a few parishes' transcripts commence in 1685 but most begin in 1700; and the archdeaconries of Cardigan and St David's have some from the end of the seventeenth century and virtually nothing for the whole of the eighteenth century, until the main series commences in 1799. All surviving transcripts are held at the National Library of Wales, those for the diocese of Bangor and Llandaff are available to view on microfiche, the originals can be seen for all other dioceses.

The transcripts were meant to serve two purposes: to safeguard against fraudulent entries and to provide duplicate entries if the parish registers were lost or destroyed at some point. Where the transcripts survive they can be an extremely valuable resource for filling in important gaps, especially if a register is missing or illegible. Occasionally, the information in the bishops' transcripts and parish registers does not correspond, or more information can be found in one than the other. It is recommended wherever possible to check both sources for information. Transcripts continued to be sent to the bishop until the 1860s; however, there are many Welsh parishes that have transcripts for much later dates. As a rule, the transcripts did not include marriage entries after the introduction of civil registration in 1837. For dates of surviving bishops' transcripts see the book by C. J. Williams and J. Watts-Williams, which is listed in the further reading section.

The outbreak of the English Civil War and the onset of the Interregnum (1642–60) saw an early form of civil registration when Oliver Cromwell introduced 'registers': 'able and honest men' who

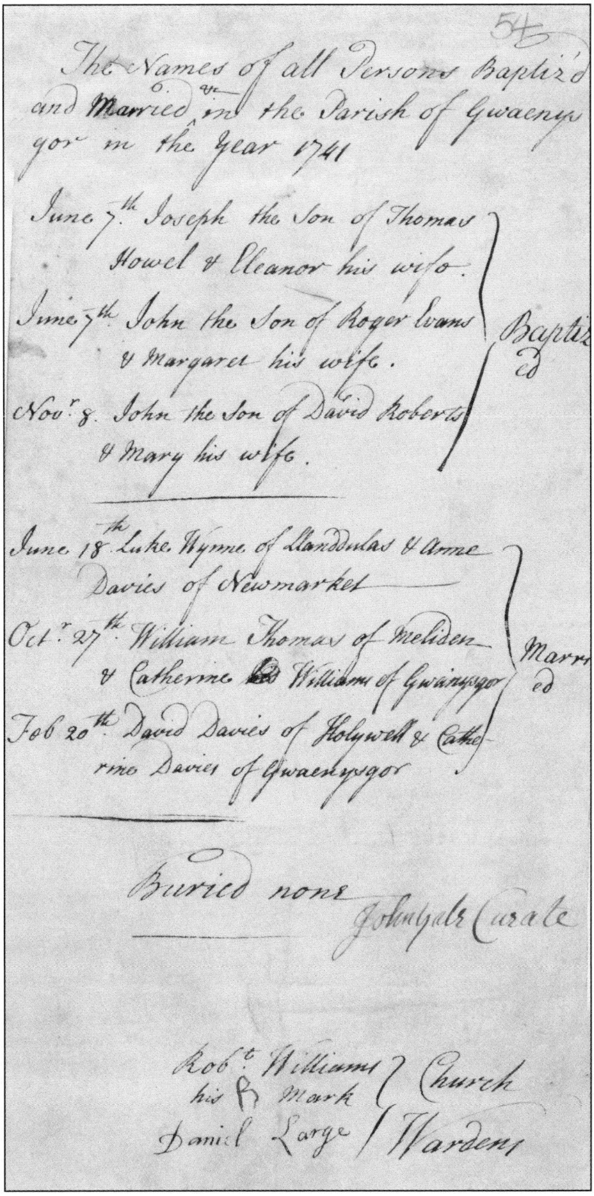

54

The Names of all Persons Baptiz'd and Married in the Parish of Gwaenysgor in the Year 1741

June 7th Joseph the Son of Thomas Howel & Eleanor his wife.

June 7th John the Son of Roger Evans & Margaret his wife.

Novr 8. John the Son of David Roberts & Mary his wife.

Baptized

June 18th Luke Wynne of Llanddulas & Anne Davies of Newmarket

Octr 27th William Thomas of Meliden & Catherine Williams of Gwaenysgor

Feb 20th David Davies of Holywell & Catherine Davies of Gwaenysgor

Married

Buried none

John Yale Curate

Robt Williams his R mark

Daniel Large

Church Wardens

Bishop's transcripts Gwaenysgor, Flintshire, 1741. (NLW)

were elected annually. Therefore, the administration of vital events was no longer undertaken by the Established Church but by civil officers. As a result, marriages took place as a civil ceremony in front of a magistrate rather than a minister. The period is often known to family historians as the 'Commonwealth gap' due to the apparent lack of vital events and the poor record keeping. With the restoration of the monarchy in 1660, an Act of Parliament legalized all the civil marriages that had taken place since 1642 and parish registers were once more used to record events.

These early registers did not have any particular order: many had all events listed chronologically for each year, some had baptisms and burials together and marriages separately, whilst others had all events listed separately for each year. It is recommended that you spend some time browsing through these early registers, as well as the bishops' transcripts, in order to familiarize yourself with the formats used. Often, baptisms or burials can be misinterpreted if they appear together. Additionally, many of these early records were written in Latin and many of the Christian names and surnames were Latinized. Therefore, when you come to look at these records, it is advisable to familiarize yourself with some basic Latin for family and local historians, in order to understand names, dates and events. The use of patronymics was also be prevalent during this period (see Chapter 2).

Prior to 1752, England and Wales used the Julian calendar, in which the year began on 25 March – or Lady Day, as it was called in many records. All entries in parish registers each year prior to 1752 ran from 25 March to 24 March. Therefore, entries prior to 1752 may be referred to as, for example, 1749/50 if the date occurs between 31 December and 25 March. As a result of an Act of Parliament in 1751/52, the Julian calendar was abandoned and the Gregorian calendar was adopted, which meant that the year ran from 1 January until 31 December.

Towards the end of the eighteenth century, additional information gradually appeared in some parish registers. The name of a dwelling was often recorded, which was very useful in Wales for distinguishing between two individuals of the same name; the use

Baptism entries 1858–60 Bodewryd parish register, Anglesey. (NLW)

of 'senior' and 'junior' was used to tell different generations apart; ages appeared on burial entries; and occasionally the names of both parents appeared on baptism entries. 1813 saw the commencement of the use of uniform pre-printed forms to record baptisms, marriages and burials. This came about as a result of Rose's Act 'for the better regulating and preserving of Parish and other Registers of Births, Baptisms and Marriages and Burials in England and Wales'. Ministers of each parish were provided with printed, bound copies of the registers and they were responsible for keeping these in a correct and proper manner.

Baptisms

The new baptism registers saw specific columns created for the recording of:

- Date of baptism
- Child's Christian name
- Parents' names
- Abode of family
- Quality, trade or profession of father
- By whom the ceremony was performed

Prior to these standard forms, often the only information recorded was the name of the child and the father's name. It must be remembered that the date of baptism is not the date of birth: baptism usually took place a few days or weeks after birth, sometimes much later. Occasionally a note will be made that the child was privately baptized, which was usually done at the home of a sick baby; the child would be publicly baptized at a later date if he/she survived. Sometimes, multiple baptisms of the children of one family took place at the same time, but this does not necessarily indicate a multiple birth because the ages of the children were not always recorded. Birth certificates and baptismal entries may not always show the same Christian names, due to the use of nicknames or variations of longer Christian names: for example, Peggy would often appear in official records as Margaret, whilst Sioni, a variation of Sion, was the Welsh version of John.

Marriages

In 1754 Hardwicke's Marriage Act was introduced 'for the better preventing of Clandestine Marriages'. There is some evidence to suggest that clandestine marriages were common throughout the seventeenth and early eighteenth century. Some of them were recorded in parish registers, but many more probably went unrecorded. From 1754 onwards, all marriages had to be preceded by the publishing of banns, or by licence, and the ceremony had to take place in the parish church where either the bride or groom was resident. Quakers and Jews were exempt from this act, but all other nonconformists were forced to marry in a church. As Jews and Quakers were not plentiful in Wales during the period between 1754 and 1837, it could be assumed that virtually all marriages that took place in Wales during this period were recorded in the parish registers. Entries had to be recorded in a separate, specially printed register and sequentially numbered in order to reduce fraudulent entries. The standard forms would include the names of both parties along with the parish, whether the couple were married by licence or banns, the date of the marriage and the names of the ministers and two witnesses.

It was legal for males aged 14 and females aged 12 to marry with the consent of parents or guardians, whilst the age for marrying without consent was 21 years. This was in force until 1929, when the lower age for marriage was raised to 16 years for both parties, but consent for those under 21 years remained until 1969, when the age was lowered to 18 years and remains the same today.

The National Library of Wales holds about 90,000 bonds and affidavits relating to marriages held in Wales between 1616 and 1837. Although they all relate to marriages by licence as opposed to marriages by banns, both types of marriages were recorded in the parish register.

Before marrying in a parish church you had to make sure there was no impediment to the marriage. The usual way to do this was by publishing banns: that is, making a public declaration that you intended to marry. The banns would be published (or announced) during the service at the parish church on three successive Sundays prior to the intended marriage. If the bride and groom lived in different parishes, the banns had to be published in both parish churches. Well-off people could avoid publicity and delay by marrying by licence. If you had a licence from the church authorities there was no need to have banns called. In Wales, a licence would usually be issued in the bishop's name.

To obtain a licence, the bridegroom would normally appear before a surrogate (a person authorized to act for the bishop's court in the granting of marriage licences) and swear an oath that he knew of no impediment to the marriage. The oath was recorded in a document known as an affidavit or allegation. Until 1823, the bridegroom and a friend would also enter into a bond: a document that obliged them to pay a sum of money. These bonds are known as marriage bonds. If an impediment to the marriage should come to light, or if the conditions of the licence should be breached, then the bridegroom and his friend would forfeit the considerable sum of money noted in the bond. Under normal circumstances the sum would not be paid. A marriage by licence had to take place in the parish where either party had their 'usual abode' in the four weeks before the marriage; this was reduced to fifteen days in 1823.

Sometimes you will find other documents filed with the bonds and affidavits, such as certificates of baptism, letters of consent or orders to issue a licence. The licences themselves are very rarely found: most have disappeared because there was no need for the clergyman or the married couple to keep the licence once the marriage had been solemnized. The following is an example of a marriage bond:

> Know all men by these Presents, that we John Hughes of Ceidio in the Parish of Rhodygeidio in the County of Anglesey, millwright and William Owen of Whaenwen in the parish of Llantrisaint in the said county farmer are holden and firmly bound unto the Right Reverend Father in God Dr Henry William by Divine Permission Lord Bishop of Bangor in the sum of two hundred pounds of good and lawful money of Great Britain to be paid unto the said Right Reverend Father, his lawful Attorney, Executors, Administrators or Assignes … Twenty first day of June in the Year of our Lord One Thousand Eight Hundred and thirteen on which Day appeared personally John Hughes of Ceidio in the Parish of Rhodygeidio

in the county of Anglesey and Diocese of Bangor millwright and being sworn in the Holy Evangelists alledged and made Oath as follows, that he is of the Age of Eight and Twenty years and upwards and a Bachelor and intends to marry Margaret Williams of Llawr tyddyn in the Parish of Bodedern in the said county and in the Diocese aforesaid aged Four and Twenty years and a singlewoman not knowing or believing any lawful Let or Impediment by Reason of any Precontract entered into before the Twenty-fifth of March, One Thousand Seven Hundred and Fifty Four, Consanguinity, Affinity or any other cause whatsoever, to hinder the said intended marriage: And he prayed a Licence to solemnize the said marriage in the Parish church of Bodedern aforesaid. In which Parish aforesaid He the said John Hughes further made oath that the said Margaret Williams hath had her usual abode for the space of Four weeks last past. (NLW, Marriage Bonds, B46/112)

If a marriage took place in Wales by licence, it is quite likely that there is an affidavit and/or bond amongst the diocesan records held at the National Library of Wales.

A rough guide to the survival of bonds and affidavits is as follows:

Diocese	Dates
Bangor	1757–1931 + a few 1691–96
Brecon (Archdeaconry)	1661–1867
Llandaff	1665–1941 with gaps
St Asaph	1690–1938 + a few 1616–89
St David's	1661–1867 + a few 1616–21

The details found in the marriage bonds index are:

- the names of the bride and groom;
- their rank or occupation;
- their marital status;
- their home parish;
- the date of the document;

- the church where the wedding was to take place;
- the type (s) of document (s) available: B – bond, A – affidavit, C – certificate, L – letter, Lic – licence, O – order;
- the call number of the document.

The National Library of Wales online index covers marriage bonds up to 1837. There is no available index to the bonds after this date, but a search can be made for the relevant documents if some indication can be given of the approximate date of the marriage. Typical entries in the index would be:

Griffith, Morgan, bach., gent., Llanystumdwy, Caernarfonshire to Morris, Jane, singlewoman, Llanystumdwy, Caernarfonshire: 1802, May 20, marriage at Llanystumdwy, marriage bond, Bangor 35/76

David, Thomas, yeoman, Lampeter, Cardiganshire to Griffith, Gwenllian, sp., Abergwili, Carmarthenshire: 1719 Feb 16, marriage at Abergwili, Carmarthenshire, marriage order, St Davids 3/55

Marriage settlements are a source of information that is often underused by family historians, which is a shame as they can contain a great deal of detail relating to ownership of property and relationships between the parties involved. It was usually families that owned property or had large sums of money that drew up these marriage settlements or prenuptial agreements.

When a couple married, the law considered that everything a woman had owned before her marriage would become the property of her husband, to use as he pleased. Marriage settlements were created in order to overcome this and would set out details of funding to provide for the wife during her husband's life and after his death. Details of settlements varied greatly and many included further provisions that were related to matters other than property. The need for marriage settlements did not change until the Married Women's Property Act of 1882, which gave married women the same legal rights as those of single women.

Marriage settlements can be found amongst family and solicitors' papers held at the National Library of Wales or at local county archive offices. Searches for possible documents and related papers should be made through the Archives Wales website and by using the online catalogue of the National Library of Wales. Enquiries can also be made at local county archive offices with regard to material that might not have been catalogued.

Many of these documents are very lengthy and can contain a great deal of detail about families and the property they owned. The following is a typical example of the people and properties involved in such a document:

> Articles of Agreement for a marriage settlement dated 13 December 1738 between 1 Maud Griffith of Duffryn in the parish of Blaenporth, co. Cards., widow and relict of Jenkin Griffith of Duffryn aforesaid, gent., deceased, Elinor Jenkins of Kilybronney in the parish of Langoedmore, co. Cards., widow and relict of Griffith Jenkins of Kilybronney, gent., eldest son and heir of the said Elinor and grandson of the said Maud; 2 John Lewes of Tredeved, co. Pembroke, gent., and Elizabeth Lewes of Tredved, spinster, youngest daughter of the said John Lewes; 3 Thomas Lewes of Tredeved, esq., Watkin Lewes, rector of Meline, co. Pembroke, clerk, Thomas Lloyd of Landgoedmore, gent., and Thomas Jenkins of Duffryn aforesaid, gent., before the marriage of the said Jonathan Jenkins and the said Elizabeth Lewes, relating to the following properties – the capital messuage and lands called Kilybronney with three messuages or parcels of lands called Tyr y Gwern Hiscock, Tyr Pen y Bryn and Tyr Bronglewyn adjoining the said capital messuage in the parish of Llangoedmore; another messuage and lands in the parish of Mount and Verwick, co. Cards., called Trekeven and a slang of land called Llain Kefen y Bettell; another messuage and lands called Tyr y Garnwen alias Tyr Pen yr Allt and a piece of land called Tyr Meredith both in the parish of Aberport, co. Cards., upon trusts as specified. (NLW, Cilgwyn Estate, 1452)

Marriage settlements can be a valuable source of additional information relating to families, especially during periods when other documentation is unavailable and/or prior to parish registers. The National Library of Wales holds settlements and agreements of marriages dating from the early 1500s and a card index is available to use in conjunction with the online catalogue.

Deaths

The new burial registers, which were introduced in 1813, show the following information:

- Name
- Abode
- When buried
- Age
- By whom ceremony was performed

The addition of age is significant, as this information is useful in tracing birth or baptism records. Once a burial or date of death has been found, other records can be searched, such as transcripts of monumental inscriptions, newspaper obituaries and even wills. Additional information that can be found in a burial record might include the names of parents in a child's record, the husband's name in a widow's record, or additional notes about the cause of death written in the margin – as is shown in the image (17) of the burial register from Llanbadarn Trefeglwys, Cardiganshire in 1864. The date of burial is not the date of death, which usually would have occurred only a few days before.

The Church of England's official role as administrator of vital events of our ancestors did not come to an end with the introduction of civil registration on 1 July 1837. They continued to record events within their own parish registers and still do so today, nearly two hundred years later. If you are unable to trace a birth, marriage or death certificate it is always worth checking parish registers, baptisms and burial entries, which can include additional information, although marriage entries from 1837 onwards follow

A page from the 1864 burial register of Llanbadarn Trefeglwys parish, Cardiganshire, with additional notes that relate to the cause of death. (NLW)

the same format as a civil marriage certificate and therefore the information should be the same.

The Church in Wales was, until its disestablishment in 1920, an integral part of the Church of England. England and Wales were divided into dioceses, each one under the administration of a bishop.

The dioceses were further divided into parishes and some larger parishes were split into several townships. The diocesan boundaries disregarded those of England and Wales. The four ancient Welsh dioceses covered the following areas:

- Bangor – Anglesey, most of Caernarfonshire, parts of Merionethshire and Montgomeryshire and the deanery of Dyffryn Clwyd in central Denbighshire.
- Llandaff – most of Glamorgan and Monmouthshire.
- St Asaph – most of Flintshire and Denbighshire, with part of Caernarfonshire, Meirionethshire, Montgomeryshire and Shropshire.
- St David's – Carmarthenshire, Cardiganshire, Pembrokeshire, Breconshire, most of Radnorshire and parts of Montgomeryshire, Glamorgan, Monmouthshire and Herefordshire.
- Hawarden in Flintshire is the only peculiar (that is, parish) exempt from episcopal jurisdiction.
- Some of the English dioceses included parts of Wales.
- Chester – parts of Flintshire and Denbighshire.
- Lichfield – parish of Penley, Flintshire and the Welsh part of Llanymynech, Shropshire.
- Hereford – parts of Montgomeryshire, Radnorshire and Monmouthshire.

In 1950, an agreement was made between the National Library of Wales and the Representative Body of the Church in Wales with regard to the collection of parish registers and other diocesan records relating to Wales. As a result, registers of approximately 1,000 Welsh parishes and chapelries were deposited at the National Library or county archive offices. The registers of Welsh parishes remaining in the Church of England have been deposited in the appropriate county archive office: Chester, Shropshire or Herefordshire.

Over the years, for conservation reasons, all original parish registers held at the National Library of Wales have been microfilmed and it is only the microfilm copies that can be viewed by the public. For dates of surviving parish registers, and associated transcripts and indexes, you should consult the book by C. J. Williams and J. Watts-Williams, which is listed in the further reading section.

The Genealogical Society of Utah, in conjunction with the National Library of Wales, the Welsh county archive offices and the Church in Wales, has recently undertaken a project to digitize all parish registers held in Welsh repositories. These are now available to view online, at Findmypast (through subscription)or free of charge at Welsh county archive offices and the National Library of Wales.

Copies of Welsh parish registers can also be consulted at county archive offices, which hold copies and originals pertaining to their own counties. The Society of Genealogists also holds a comprehensive collection of microfilm and microfiche copies of Welsh parish registers. The Church of Jesus Christ of Latter Day Saints (LDS) holds the most extensive – although incomplete – collection of copies of Welsh parish registers outside the National Library of Wales. These have been transcribed and indexed, and they can be accessed at the Familysearch website. As is inevitable with transcripts, they will contain errors; so although they can be useful for gathering data more quickly, remember to check any information found against the original registers.

Further reading
Williams, C. J. and Watts-Williams, John, *Cofrestri Plwyf Cymru/Parish Registers of Wales* (National Library of Wales, 2000)

Websites
Archives Wales **www.archiveswales.org.uk**
Association of Family History Societies of Wales
www.fhswales.org.uk
Familysearch **www.familysearch.org/**
Findmypast **www.findmypast.co.uk/articles/world-records/**
    search-all-uk-records/special-collections/the-wales-collection
National Library of Wales **http://cat.llgc.org.uk**

Chapter 7

NONCONFORMITY

Nonconformity became widespread in Wales during the seventeenth century and increased further from the eighteenth century onwards. A nonconformist was someone who did not conform to the beliefs of the Established Church; nonconformists were also referred to as Dissenters.

After the restoration of the Monarchy in 1660 and an attempt to enforce membership of the Church, there was great resistance to what was known as the Clarendon Code. The code ended toleration of dissenting religions in England and Wales by re-establishing the supremacy of the Anglican Church and imposing severe penalties on those who refused to conform to the Established Church. As a result, for many years nonconformist meetings were held in secret all over Wales. During the seventeenth century, the building of chapels and the keeping of any records was very rare and few of either have survived from this early period of nonconformity.

The Toleration Act of 1689 allowed freedom of worship to nonconformists who pledged themselves to the oaths of Allegiance and Supremacy and permitted them to build their own meeting houses and appoint their own ministers. From the mid-eighteenth century they also began to keep registers. However, the Act did not extend to Catholics and Unitarians, with the result that their records tend to begin much later.

Hardwicke's Marriage Act of 1753 was the first legislation to affect the keeping of nonconformist registers. All marriages between 1754 and 1837 (except for those of the Quakers and Jews) had to take place within the Established Church – even if the bride and groom were of nonconformist denomination – and, as a result, virtually every marriage in Wales was recorded in the parish registers. However, there was no such requirement for baptisms; therefore, on the whole, nonconformist baptisms do not appear in the parish records. Amongst the many types of nonconformist records there are: birth/baptism, marriage and burial registers; manuscript lists for members; contribution books for individual chapels; printed annual reports from 1880 onwards; and denominational periodicals. The difficulty faced by researchers is the fact that there was no central body for nonconformist religions in Wales, even though a variety of denominations emerged during the seventeenth and eighteenth centuries namely: Congregationalists, Independents, Calvinistic Methodists (Presbyterians), Baptists, Quakers, Unitarians and numerous other smaller groups.

Towards the end of the eighteenth century it became apparent that nonconformist registers were not deemed to be as legal as the Anglican registers. The consequent agitation, and the increase in

Baptism register of Capel Celyn CM, Llanycil, Merionethshire, 1811–20 showing some of the information found in a nonconformist register. (NLW, CMA III/EZ1/59/1)

Mother's Parish before Marriage.	When Child Born.	In what Parish Born.	When Baptized.	Where Baptized.	By whom Baptized.	Remarks.
Llan y cil	Febr. 12. 1811	Llan y cil	Febr. 26. 1811	Penbryn fawr	Mr J. Lloyd	
Llan y cil	November 18. 1812	Llan y cil	Novem. 28. 1812	Do	Mr J. Lloyd	
Llan y cil	Novem. 25.	Llan y cil	December 24. 1815	Do	Mr J. Lloyd	
Llanfor	Jan. 18. 1817	Llanfor	Febr. 5. 1817	Penbryn	Mr W. Jones	
Llan y cil	Jan. 24. 1817	Llanfor	Febr. 5. 1817	Penbryn	Mr W. Jones	
Llan y cil	October 22. 1818	Llan y cil	October 31. 1818	Denbryy	William Havard	
Llan y cil	October 24. 1818	Llan y cil	October 31. 1818	Do	William Havard	
Llan y cil	Janur. 10. 1817	Llan y cil	Janur. 24. 1817	Penbryn	Mr J. Lloyd	
Llan y cil	April 18. 1819	Llan y cil	April 20. 1819	Ammodd	Mr Jones	
Llan y cil	August 3. 1819	Llanfor	August 15. 1819	Penbryn	John Humphrey	
Llanfor	September 21. 1819	Llanfor	November 27. 1819	Penbryn	William Roberts	
Llan y cil	Janur. 1. 1819	Llan y cil	Janur. 6. 1819	Graygronw	Mr J. Lloyd	
Llan y cil	November 27. 1819	Llan y cil	December 6. 1819	Maes y dail	Mr J. Lloyd	
Trawsmynydd	Febr. 25. 1819	Llan y cil	March 8. 1819	Maes y dail	Mr J. Lloyd	
Trawsmynydd	Novem. 6. 1820	Llan y cil	Novem 18. 1820	Maes y dail	Mr J. Lloyd	
Trawsmynydd	May 28. 1819	Llay y cil	June 6. 1819	Penbryn	Mechel Roberts	
Llan y cil	September 28. 1820	Llan y cil	October 4. 1820	Do	Mr J. Lloyd	
Llan y cil	July 20. 1821	Llan y cil	July 22. 1821	Capel Celyn	John Roberts	
Llan y cil	October 24. 1822	Llan y cil	October 31. 1822	Bwlch y bwart	John Lewis	

nonconformist Members of Parliament in 1832, resulted in the implementation of the Civil Registration Act, which came into force in England and Wales in 1837. From 1 July of that year, marriages could be solemnized in a nonconformist chapel, as well as in the parish church or civil register office, as long as a civil registrar was present to witness the ceremony.

In 1836, a commission was set up to enquire into the state, authenticity and custody of every birth/baptism, marriage and death/burial register in England and Wales, other than parochial records. As a result, chapels were required to hand over the registers in their possession so that they could be deposited with the Registrar General. Of the 3,630 received from all over England and Wales, the majority would be acceptable in a court of law, as they could be consulted by the public and the Registrar General could supply certificates from them. This was seen to be a great triumph for the nonconformists. Microfilm copies of all the registers relating to Wales are now held at The National Archives in classes RG4, RG6 and RG8 and can be viewed at the National Library of Wales. In addition, most county archive offices hold microfilms of those relevant to their area. These can also be searched free of charge online through The National Archives website, but you will be required to buy credits to view the full records and the images of the original pages.

With the introduction of civil registration in 1837, there was no legal obligation for the nonconformists to continue keeping registers, but the vast majority continued to do so out of habit, alongside the registers of communicants and members. The use of the Welsh language can frequently be seen in the registers of the late nineteenth and early twentieth centuries – in fact, many were written in Welsh throughout, with no English translation. Staff at the National Library of Wales or local county archive offices may well be able help with deciphering records.

If you are unable to find your ancestors in the parish records, it can be worth looking at the records of the nonconformist chapels. Unfortunately, chapel records have not been as safely and conscientiously kept as the records of the Established Church. Nonconformist papers are stored in various locations, including the

National Library of Wales, The National Archives in Kew and the county archive offices; additionally, some records are still in the possession of the ministers and chapel officers or even in private hands. For surviving registers held in repositories throughout Wales, see Dafydd Ifans' book and also the Capeli Cymru (Chapels of Wales) database, which is in the South Reading Room at the National Library of Wales.

During the 1980s, the National Library of Wales compiled a comprehensive index to all the nonconformist causes that had ever existed in Wales, noting the location of any surviving records where possible. This database, the Capeli Cymru, lists 5,500 chapels: but, of these, only 1,350 have registers in a public repository. The database is only available to search in the South Reading Room at the National Library of Wales and includes all records pertaining to

Alltyblaca Unitarian Chapel, Llanwenog, Cardiganshire c.1885. (NLW, John Thomas Collection)

chapels, rather than just the registers. Information relating to a particular chapel can include registers, records, accounts, contributions, annual reports, Sunday school records, history, pictures, deeds, plans, societies and charities. However, it is rare for records for all classes to exist for a particular chapel, as survival of such documentation varies greatly.

The information from the database formed the basis of Dafydd Ifans' book, *Nonconformist Registers of Wales*, which refers to the main Welsh Christian denominations: the Calvinistic Methodists (Presbytarians), the Baptists, the Congregationalists and the Wesleyan Methodists. There are also many smaller denominations included, such as Quakers, Unitarians and the Countess of Huntingdon's Connexion. The book does not refer to or give details of Catholic registers, but details of these have been included in Michael Gandy's book, *Catholic Missions and Registers 1700–1880*. However, *Nonconformist Registers of Wales* does show the Welsh and English name of each parish: these are listed alphabetically under the pre-1974 counties; the name of the chapel; the denomination; the type of register, with covering dates and the locations where they it was held; and the OS map reference number. For example:

LAMPETER/LLANBEDR PONT STEFFAN Soar *Cong.*
OS ref. SN57684795
C 1872–87 **NLW**

LAMPETER/LLANBEDR PONT STEFFAN St Thomas *W*
OS ref. SN57724804
C 1835–1931 **NLW** 1839–1973 **NLW** B1835–1931 **NLW**

Unlike parish registers – the entries for which were written on printed pages, in bound volumes, for marriages (from 1754) and baptisms and burials (from 1813) – nonconformist registers tended to be more haphazard and no pressure was put upon the denominations to keep such records and to later pass them to public repositories. Furthermore, as the depositing of nonconformist registers has been largely voluntary in Wales, only a small number have made their way to any of the archive repositories previously mentioned.

Denominational periodicals often contain a section for births, marriages and deaths. Although primarily of value for the particulars of members of the denomination in question, notes on members of other denominations may also appear in such publications. The first of these to be published, as a result of the eighteenth-century religious revival, was *Trysorfa Ysprydol* (Spiritual Treasury) in 1799. It was a way of supplying itinerant preachers and Sunday school teachers with information and also provided reading material for pupils. Many more periodicals followed during the nineteenth century: it is worth remembering that they were usually published in the Welsh language:

Yr Eurgrawn Wesleyaidd (1809 Wesleyan Methodists)
Seren Gomer (1818 Baptist)
Y Drysorfa (1831 Calvinistic Methodist)
Y Dysgedydd (1832 Independents)
Y Diwygiwr (1835 Congregational)
Yr Ymofynydd (1847 Unitarian)

The Welsh Calvinistic Methodists, now known as the Presbyterian Church of Wales, have records in their collections that date from early on in the development of the movement. The Calvinistic Methodist Archive has been in existence since a General Assembly decision in 1934, and all relevant records have to be deposited in the central archive at the National Library of Wales. The records consist of three major groups: the Trevecka College group, the Bala College group and the General Collection. The first deals mainly with records pertaining to the development of Methodism in Wales and the archives of Howell Harris, who was a Methodist reformer, revivalist and leader in Wales. Included in this group are diaries, letters and accounts relating to Welsh Methodism.

The Bala College group deals mainly with the development of Methodism in the nineteenth century: its spread through Wales, the formation of the Confession of Faith in 1823 and the denomination's separation from the Established Church in 1911.

The General Collection is the largest group, with over 30,000 items listed. The records in this group are of great value to those who have any nonconformist ancestors in their family. The records cover association and district meetings, colleges, individual chapels and personal archives of ministers and other lay members. In addition, the Foreign Mission archive covers the missionary work of the Church in north-east India and contains records that date from the 1840s.

Descriptions of all the records of the Presbyterian Church of Wales can be searched by using the online catalogues of the National Library of Wales. Further information relating to the Presbyterian Church of Wales can be found on their website.

The earliest known surviving nonconformist register is the Ilston Book, which contains records of the Baptist Church established at Ilston, Swansea in 1649: the earliest Baptist church in Wales. The original register is held at the John Carter Brown Library in Brown University, Providence, Rhode Island. The founder of the university, John Miles, took it with him to America c.1662–3, where he established a further church in 1667, in Swansea, Massachusetts. The National Library of Wales holds a facsimile copy that is bound in two volumes (NLW Mss 9108–9D). As the Baptists did not perform infant baptisms, they tended to register births and baptisms, but the latter are usually records of adult baptisms and often do not include the age of the individual concerned. Such records are combined with other records, such as lists of members or confessions of faith made by founding congregations. Examples of Baptist chapel registers can be found at the National Library of Wales: Rhydwilym, 1667–1823 (NLW, Minor Deposit 127A); Llangloffan, 1745–1787 (NLW, Minor Deposit 412A); and Blaen-y-waun, 1794–1815 (NLW, Minor Deposit 505B) written completely in Welsh. The following are examples of entries found in the early Rhydwilym register:

Elizabeth Nicolas and Lettice Nicolas her sister, of Vrechva
was baptized July the 13 1822
Thomas John of Vrechva was excluded August the 11 1822
Morris Nicolas was restored Sepber 7 1822
Mary Harri Maenclochog was restored at Rhydwilim
November the 31 1822

The Welsh Methodist (Wesleyan) Archive, also known as the 'Amgueddfa'r Hen Gapel Tre'r Ddol' Collection is located at the National Library of Wales. It is by no means a complete collection of Wesleyan material, but it does includes a varied collection from ministers, circuit records and private donations. Within the collection are early circuit stewards' account books from Pwllheli, 1810–16, and Cardigan,1810–38; an account book from a day school at Aberystwyth, 1844–53; and a copy of the Machynlleth circuit baptisms register, which commences in 1808. The second Cilgwyn register book, also within the collection, has entries from 1770, which pre-dates the establishment of Welsh Wesleyan Methodism; it was not until 1864 that this chapel joined the Lampeter circuit. The first entries from the register are as follows:

> John son of Evan Thos James & Elizth his wife was born at CefnbysYstrad Parish Feby 9th 1770 Baptized March 18th 1770 by the Revd Timothy Davies

> Daniel son of Evan Thos James & Elizth his wife was born at CefnbysYstrad Parish May 27th 1773 Baptized June 10th 1773 Rev Daniel Gronow

The registers of the Wesleyan Methodists cover a circuit rather than one specific chapel. An example is that of Peniel Chapel, Llandysul, which covers an area in South Cardiganshire and areas in North Carmarthenshire and Pembrokeshire. Some Wesleyan circuits on the border with England may be held in English record offices; for instance, some that relate to Montgomeryshire are in Shrewsbury, whilst a number of registers that pertain to Radnorshire are in Hereford and some for Monmouthshire are in Gloucestershire. It is worth remembering that all Wesleyan circuits cover a larger area than a particular parish and can cover areas in other counties.

The contents of the Welsh Methodist (Wesleyan) archives can be searched through the online catalogue of the National Library of Wales or through the Archives Wales website; local county archive offices should also be consulted with regard to the records they hold for local chapels.

With the restoration of the monarchy in 1660, the Quakers found themselves liable to be prosecuted and treated with hostility; as a result, many were attracted to the religious freedom offered by the new colonies in North America, especially Pennsylvania. The Quakers or Society of Friends were amongst the first nonconformist denominations to keep regular registers; however, as they did not have baptisms, they kept birth registers and burial registers – and of course marriage registers, as they were not included in Hardwicke's Marriage Act of 1753 and were therefore exempt from having to marry in a parish church. A number of early quarterly meetings of the Quakers in Wales and the border counties with England, which occurred between 1646 and 1838, are amongst those deposited with the registrar general and are now housed at The National Archives in Kew (RG 6/631-709). Microfilm copies of these records can be viewed at the National Library of Wales, or online at The National Archives, as previously mentioned. The Glamorgan Archives is recognized by Friends House in London as the repository for Welsh Quaker records and many records relating to the border counties are held at the Hereford Record Office.

The Society of Friends in Wales consists of individual congregations that are grouped together regionally and the regions hold monthly meetings. These regions form part of divisions and the divisions hold quarterly meetings. For much of the time, there were two main divisions, which covered north Wales and south Wales. The north Wales division also included Shropshire, England. The collection held at Glamorgan Archives covers the period between 1659 and 1997 and, in addition to monthly and quarterly minutes, it includes preparative minutes, printed material, licences and memorials, school records, deeds, plans, contracts and certificates of removal. For a more detailed description of the records that are held, visit the Archives Wales website or contact Glamorgan Archives.

The earliest Welsh Catholic register, for Holywell, Flintshire, dates from 1698 onwards. The first deposit of Roman Catholic records from the Archdiocese of Cardiff, which covers the period from 1850 to 1916, includes correspondence; sermons; addresses; papers relating to missions, religious orders, school and diocesan affairs; as well as three registers from Llan-narth, Monmouthshire for 1781–1933. This collection has been deposited at the National Library of Wales. County archive offices should be checked for other Roman Catholic records along with the Archives Wales website and Michael Gandy's publication, as previously mentioned.

Further reading

Breed, G. R., *My Ancestors Were Baptists* (SOG, 1995)

Clifford, David J. H., *My Ancestors Were Congregationalists* (SOG, 1997)

Gandy, Michael, *Catholic Missions and Registers 1700–1880 Volume 3, Wales and the West of England* (London, 1993)

Ifans, Dafydd, *Cofrestri Anghydffurfiol Cymru/Nonconformist Registers of Wales* (NLW, 1994)

Leary, W. *My Ancestors were Methodists* (SOG, 1990)

Owen, D. Huw, *The Chapels of Wales* (Seren, 2012)

Websites

Ancestry **www.ancestry.co.uk**

Archives Wales **www.archiveswales.org.uk**

Association of Family History Societies of Wales **www.fhswales.org.uk**

Familysearch **www.familysearch.org**

Findmypast **www.findmypast.co.uk**

National Library of Wales **www.cat.llgc.org.uk**

Presbyterian Church in Wales **www.ebcpcw.org.uk**

The National Archives **www.bmdregisters.co.uk**

Chapter 8

PARISH CHEST RECORDS

Having used parish records such as baptism, marriage and burial registers to trace your ancestors, you can delve further into other records held within parish chests, in order to put more flesh on the bones of your research. It is surprising how many of our ancestors may have been mentioned at one time or another amongst the vestry minutes, accounts from churchwardens or records from overseers of the poor. They could have been mentioned because they could needed to ask for relief as the result of difficult circumstances, or they may have been one of the tradesmen or craftsmen, or other inhabitants of the parish, who provided a service to the church vestry at some point.

From the sixteenth century until the mid-nineteenth century, the parish was responsible for numerous aspects of administration, which included providing for the poor, responsibility for highways and other aspects of law and order. Following the 1601 Poor Law Act, two overseers of the poor were appointed every year from the wealthier householders of the parish. Along with the churchwardens, the overseers were responsible for the relief of the poor and were required to collect the poor rate – which was set at the vestry meetings – and keep accounts of payments such as rent, clothes and other expenses relating to the poor. Individuals who received relief are more often than not named within the accounts and some people can be traced through the vestry records from the cradle to the grave.

Records that can be found in the parish chest and which will be of assistance and interest to family historians are:

- • Vestry minutes
- • Churchwardens' accounts

- Overseers of the poor accounts
- Settlement certificates and removal orders
- Apprenticeship records
- Bastardy records

However, as with parish registers, survival of records varies from parish to parish and all the above records will not be found for each parish. Surviving Welsh records are located at the county archive offices that hold the corresponding parish registers. There are also records held in various collections within the National Library of Wales; therefore, it is also worth checking the online catalogue for possibilities. Many of the early records of vestry minutes and accounts can be found amongst the pages of parish registers.

The most important of these records are the vestry minutes. The vestry was not only open to Anglicans, but to all parishioners. Dissenters were also able to take part and make decisions within a vestry. The vestry meeting was usually chaired by the parish incumbent and attended by the ratepayers of the parish, such as farmers and other wealthy men of standing . As the name suggests, the meetings were usually held at the church vestry; however, it was not uncommon for the meeting to open at the vestry, but continue at the local inn. The accounts would often include payments for bread, cheese and ale that had been provided at these meetings.

> At a Parish meeting held this 30th Day of April 1794 we the Church Wardens, Overseers of the poor and several other Inhabitants of the Parish of Landilotalybont Do Settle and Agree that there shall be a quart of ale to every Inhabitant that shall attend Vesteries in each Vestry this present year.
> (WGAS, P/108/8, Llandeilo Talybont Vestry Minute book p.104)

Decisions taken in these meetings included the setting of the amount of the poor rate, the church rate and the highway rate, which all occupiers of houses and land within the parish had to pay. The vestry decided on the value of each property and ratepayers paid a certain number of pence in the pound depending on the property's worth. Decisions were also made on all manner of other issues that had been brought to the vestry's attention, especially with regard to the poorer members of the parish.

Two churchwardens were appointed at Easter each year and their accounts provide a record of the upkeep of the church. The vestry was responsible for setting the church rate, but it was the churchwardens' duty to collect the money and to keep an account of any payments made to tradesmen and craftsmen in relation to the building itself and its everyday running. You may find an ancestor listed in the accounts stating his occupation: a piece of information that may not have been recorded in the parish registers or elsewhere.

Other payments found in the accounts of the churchwardens and overseers of the poor are: details of bastardy, apprenticeships, payments for vermin and highways. These accounts are not always recorded separately, but can often be found within the vestry minutes.

A good example of a comprehensive vestry book is that of Lampeter, 1777–1803 (Lampeter Parochial Records 1). The original is held at the Carmarthenshire Archive Service, but a digital version of the whole book can be seen on the National Library of Wales website. http://www.llgc.org.uk/index.php?id=vestrybooklampeterparochial

The following is an extract from the accounts within the volume:

An Acct of the Disbursements of Evan Jenkins and David Davies Churchwardens. In the Repairation of the Church from Easter (April 18) 1778 to Easter (April 4th) 1779

Paid to Jenkins Thomas the Mason for whitewashing	0 3 0
Paid Josiah Jones for painting the church doors and churchyard gate	0 6 0
Paid to Evan John for the sd shutters	0 3 0
Paid to John Jenkin the Smith 4 hinges and other Iron work for the church	0 4 5
Paid to Wm Davd Davies for a Lock	0 0 7
Paid to Evan David Smith for a new spade	0 3 0
Paid to David William for mending benches	0 1 3

The 1662 Act of Settlement stated that each person should have a parish of settlement in the event that they needed to apply for parish relief. This parish would be responsible for funding the relief that the individual or his/her family would require. An individual would be entitled to poor relief in several ways:

- By holding a public office
- By paying the poor rate
- Being employed within the parish for twelve months or more
- By undertaking an apprenticeship within a parish
- By paying rent of £10 per annum on a property

A wife would gain settlement in the same parish as her husband and a child would also gain settlement in the parish of his/her father. If a pregnant woman was not entitled to settlement from the parish she was living in prior to the child's birth, attempts were often made to remove her from that parish because an illegitimate child's place of settlement would be the parish where he/she was born. The 1697 Settlement Act stated that individuals entering another parish could do so on production of a settlement certificate that had been provided by their parish and which showed that their parish would accept responsibility if the person fell on hard times. Decisions relating to settlements and their outcomes were often recorded within the vestry minutes; this was the case for the son of Stephen Abel, as recorded in the Lampeter Vestry Book:

> 21st April 1790 Necessity urged the Parishrs to meet this day in order to settle the child of Stephen Abel as the mother was buried this evening – and so have ordered the child to the care of Davies of Cwmhenryd for 1/6d week, until intelligence can be had from his Father from London.

By 17 December of the same year, an application had been made for a warrant of complaint with regard to Stephen Abel Morgan, who had allowed a child to become a burden on the parish without having gained legal settlement. It was agreed that Enoch Nathaniel of Llanwenog would go to London to execute the warrant and compel Stephen Abel to make an affidavit. Relief payments and items of clothing for Abel's son appear throughout the accounts from 1791 to 1798, but on 29 October 1798 it was:

> Agreed with Evan Evans Abergranell the present Chwarden & Overseer of the Poor to keep and maintain Wm son of Stephen Abel for the term of seven years, The Parishrs have allowd a suit of cloaths and two shirts for him and no more.

Settlement papers can include great detail, sometimes naming all members of the family, their places of abode and their employment details, in order to determine the parish of settlement. Therefore, if they are available to you, settlement papers can be an invaluable source for researching your ancestors. In the settlement examination of William Davies, who lived in the town of Oswestry on 17 July 1818, but required settlement in Llanwddyn, Montgomeryshire, it states that:

> He was born in the Parish of Hirnant in the County of Montgomery that he is about forty-five Years of Age. That about four years ago he rented a farm called Garthwlch in the Parish of Llanwthin the the County of Montgomery at the annual Rent of forty Pounds and rented the same for 3 years successively Examinant is married and has 5 children at home (viz)[William aged 19 crossed out] John aged 15 David agred 12 Catherine 10 Edward aged 8 and Elizabeth aged 5 or thereabouts. (NLW, Ms 21845E, p.35)

Once it was decided that an individual was not entitled to settlement within a parish, a removal order by the Justice of the Peace was made and they would be returned to their original parish of settlement. The removal orders can sometimes be found on a printed form with the name, places, dates and other relevant information filled in by the Justice of the Peace's clerk:

John Roberts Catherine his wife Robert their son aged four years and upwards and Catherine their daughter aged one year and upwards have come to inhabit in the said Parish of Llanuwchllyn not having gained legal settlement there . . . now chargeable to the said Parish of Llanuwchllyn ... we do likewise adjudge that the lawful settlement of them ... is in the said parish of Llanwddyn the said County of Montgomery ... fifth day of May in the year of our Lord one thousand seven hundred and Eighty four. (NLW, Ms 21845E, p.5)

The 1732/33 Settlement Act stated that bastard children should be provided for by the father. Therefore, the vestries would go to great lengths to compel a mother to name the father of a child that had been or would be born out of wedlock and would then insist that the father signed a bastardy bond, so that the unmarried mother and the child would not become chargeable to the parish. The father would then be responsible for paying for the birth of the child and the upkeep of both. Unmarried mothers were not always prepared to name the father and without relatives to help with the burden it fell to parishioners; evidence of this can be found in vestry minutes and accounts of payments and assistance given to illegitimate children and their mothers.

From the age of 7, the pauper children of the parish could be apprenticed to local tradesmen or craftsmen, who would maintain them for a set number of years, usually until the age of 21. The intention was that the child would be less of a burden on the ratepayers and would potentially learn a trade. The child would became a member of that family for the duration of the apprenticeship. An indenture was drawn up, two copies were made on one piece of paper, which was duly signed by the overseer, the churchwardens, the child's master and two Justices of the Peace. This document was then cut with an uneven edge so that they could be matched together at a later date if necessary, in order to prevent any forgery. Later indentures may appear on pre-printed forms with the necessary details filled in. One copy was kept in the parish chest and the other was passed to the master and eventually given to the apprentice on completion of his/her apprenticeship. Indentures were not always produced and very few have survived in parish chests, but details of apprenticeships can be found intermittently within vestry minutes. The catalogues of county archive offices, Archives Wales and the National Library of Wales should be checked for copies that might be located amongst personal and estate papers, as well as within parochial record collections.

Further reading
Humphrey-Smith, Cecil, *The Phillimore Atlas and Index to Parish Registers* (Phillimore, 2002)

Tate, W. E., *The Parish Chest* (3rd edn, Cambridge University Press, 2008)

Williams, C. J. and John Watts-Williams, *Cofrestri Plwyf Cymru/Parish Registers of Wales* (NLW, 2000)

Websites
Archives Wales **www.archiveswales.org.uk**

Association of Family History Societies of Wales **www.fhswales.org.uk**

National Library of Wales **www.cat.llgc.org.uk**

Chapter 9

WILLS AND OTHER PROBATE RECORDS

Wills, letters of administration and other probate records provide invaluable historical and genealogical information, not only for the family historian but also for social historians and local historians. Wills can be a mine of information about the deceased's life, immediate relatives, friends and colleagues. However, it must be realized that, for most individuals, neither a will nor any other document of administration ever existed. Today, someone may consider making a will in midlife by consulting a solicitor, but until the mid-nineteenth century, making a will tended to be a last-minute consideration: a way of tidying affairs in the last few days, or even hours, of life.

The testator would name the executor of his/her will and it was the duty of this person to obtain legal permission to administer the estate; in other words, they would need to be granted 'probate'. If someone died without making a will or the will was invalid for any reason, that person would have died 'intestate'. In this situation, the next of kin could obtain letters of administration to allow them to distribute the estate if necessary. However, if the family settled the estate amongst themselves, there would be no paperwork within the probate records, but it could still be worth checking any relevant solicitors' papers held at the local county archive offices or the National Library of Wales. Probate was often granted within a few months and usually within a year of death.

Until 1858, making a will was considered to be a religious duty. Proving wills and the granting of letters of administration was the responsibility of ecclesiastical courts, each having its own area of jurisdiction. Which court had jurisdiction in any given case was

The will of John Watkins of the parish of St Michael, Brecon, Breconshire. (NLW, BR 1746/28)

determined largely by the place of death and the extent and location of the estate of the deceased. Wills were usually proved in the episcopal consistory court (the diocesan or bishop's court). If the estate comprised goods in two or more dioceses within the same province, probate was granted in either of the two provincial courts of the Archbishop of York and the Archbishop of Canterbury. The prerogative court of the Archbishop of York (PCY) administered the northern province (the northern dioceses of England, which included the southern detachment of Flint), whilst the prerogative court of the Archbishop of Canterbury (PCC) covered the southern province (the southern dioceses of Engand and Wales). If the deceased had held goods in both provinces, probate was undertaken by the PCC, which had overriding jurisdiction throughout England and Wales. Online access to the indexes and documents can be made through The National Archives website or, alternatively, the National Library of Wales holds microfilm copies of PCC wills from 1730 to 1858. The PCC wills include those of Welsh people living overseas and in the services, as well as those who held property in more than one county. The index is well worth checking if a will cannot be found elsewhere.

The right to grant probate was also held by certain church and secular courts; these were called peculiars because they were 'of peculiar or exempt jurisdiction', that is, they were outside the authority of the archdeacon or bishop. There was only one peculiar in Wales, that of Hawarden, Flintshire, which had jurisdiction in the parish of Hawarden only.

All pre-1858 probate records relating to Wales have been deposited at the National Library of Wales and comprise those of the episcopal consistory courts of St Asaph, Bangor, St David's and Llandaff; the consistory court of the archdeaconry of Brecon; the peculiar of Hawarden; and the Welsh wills proved at the episcopal consistory court of Chester. There were no ecclesiastical courts in Wales below the diocesan level. In probate matters, the consistory court of the archdeaconry of Brecon, one of the four archdeaconries of the diocese of St David's, acted as the diocesan court in a local capacity.

In tracing a pre-1858 wills/administration, the first step is to establish in which court the grant might have been made and where that court's records are held. Since probate jurisdictions did not always follow county boundaries, this can sometimes prove difficult, especially with regard to parishes bordering England and Wales.

Information concerning the probate courts that had jurisdiction in Wales, the counties and parishes they covered, and the dates of surviving records is given below. Two indispensable guides to probate records in general are *Probate Jurisdictions: Where to look for Wills* and *Wills and other Probate Records*. The series of county/parish maps published by the Institute of Heraldic and Genealogical Studies, in Canterbury, Kent, is very useful for showing the pre-1858 ecclesiastical jurisdictions.

The following is a brief summary of the position in Wales:

Probate Court	Jurisdiction (counties)
St Asaph	Most of Denbighshire and Flintshire; parts of Caernarfonshire, Merionethshire, Montgomeryshire and Shropshire
Bangor	Bangor, Anglesey; most of Caernarfonshire; parts of Denbighshire, Merionethshire and Montgomeryshire
St Davids	Cardiganshire, Carmarthenshire and Pembrokeshire; a part of Glamorganshire (deanery of Gower)
Llandaff	Most of Glamorganshire and Monmouthshire
Brecon	Breconshire; most of Radnorshire; parts of Monmouthshire, Montgomeryshire and Herefordshire
Hawarden	Parish of Hawarden, Flintshire
Chester	Parts of Flintshire and Denbighshire (one parish: Holt)
Hereford. (This group is housed at the Herefordshire Record Office)	Parts of Monmouthshire, Montgomeryshire, and Radnorshire. This court also had jurisdiction in those parishes which were partly in Shropshire and partly in Montgomeryshire (i.e. Alberbury, Mainstone and Worthen)

The pre-1858 records at the National Library of Wales cover the whole of Wales except for fifteen border parishes that came within the jurisdiction of the episcopal consistory court of Hereford, but they include seventeen English parishes which came under Welsh courts.

The main types of probate records are the will, the administration bond and the inventory. Until the end of the eighteenth century, the

The inventory of John Watkins of the parish of St Michael, Brecon, Breconshire. (NLW, BR 1746/28)

ecclesiastical courts insisted on receiving copies of the inventories, but few survive amongst probate records after this date. They can be invaluable in giving an insight into our ancestor's possessions before and during the eighteenth century. Associated documents that occasionally accompany the main records include executors' and administrators' accounts, and documents such as deposition papers and bonds of tuition and curation.

The original wills and administration bonds generally survive from about 1600 except in the case of Bangor, from which very few have survived prior to 1635. There are, however, a few extant records in original or copy form dating back to the latter half of the sixteenth century. The earliest surviving volumes of register copy wills are for St Asaph (from 1565) and Brecon (from 1543) both pre-dating the surviving original records. During the Interregnum, the local courts ceased to function, with resultant gaps in the Bangor and St Asaph records between 1648 and 1660, and in Brecon and Carmarthen (St David's diocese) between 1653 and 1660. Despite this, some wills, mainly for Glamorgan, were proved during this period at Llandaff. The records of the court of civil commission, which functioned during the Commonwealth, are filed at The National Archives with those of the PCC.

Probate act books are available for all the courts (except for Bangor and Brecon and for the Welsh wills proved at Chester), but the series that have survived are incomplete. The pre-1858 wills have been indexed and free access is available to the digital images of these wills through the National Library of Wales website

The following is a brief summary of the holdings for each court that gives covering dates only. Gaps in the series have not been noted.

St Asaph	Original wills etc., 1557–1858. Register copy wills 1521–1709. Ms indexes, 1583–1857.
Bangor	Original wills etc., 1576–1858. (There are very few wills before 1635). Register copy wills and administrations, 1790, 1851–8. Published index to pre-1700 records. Ms indexes, 1700–1858.

St David's Original wills etc., 1556–1858. Register copy
wills, 1703–1858. Ms indexes, 1600–1858
(archdeaconries of St David's (Pembrokeshire),
Cardigan and Carmarthen). The archdeaconries
are roughly equivalent to the historic counties,
but the archdeaconry of Cardigan included a
good number of north Pembrokeshire and some
Carmarthenshire parishes, and the
archdeaconry of Carmarthen included twenty-
three Glamorgan parishes and the deanery of
Gower.

Llandaff Original wills etc., 1568–1857. Register copy
wills, 1695-1844. Ms indexes, 1575–1857.

Brecon Original wills etc., 1557–1857. Register copy
wills, 1543–1858. Published index to pre-1660
records. Ms indexes, 1660–1857.

Hawarden Original wills etc., 1554–1858. Printed index,
1554–1800 in Publications of Flintshire
Historical Society, Vol. IV. Ms indexes, 1752–1857.

Chester Original wills etc., 1521–1858. Typescript
indexes, 1521–1857. Printed indexes, 1545–1837
in publications of The Record Society of
Lancashire and Cheshire.

In 1858, responsibility for probate was transferred from the complex system of church courts to a simpler system of civil probate registries. The search for a post-1858 will has become comparatively easy because since 12 January 1858, wills and administrations in England and Wales have been proved and granted in either the Principal Registry of the Family Division, or the appropriate district registry, with a copy being sent to the Probate Registry in London; as a result, any will proved from 1858 to the present day can be found in one place. Until 1941, the district registries made a second copy of the will which was entered and bound into volumes of register copy wills. It is these volumes of copy wills from the district registries with jurisdiction in Wales that constitute the post-1858 probate records held at the National Library of Wales. A list of Welsh district registries can be found in Appendix 7.

The post-1858 records comprise those from the district registries at St Asaph, Bangor, Carmarthen, Llandaff and Hereford. The exception is Shrewsbury, which covered Montgomeryshire. It should be noted that the jurisdictions reflect the territorial position contemporary with the period of the records: that is, from 1858 to 1941, rather than as they are currently. Territorial jurisdiction was abolished in 1926 and the registries at St Asaph and Hereford were closed in 1928.

District registry	Jurisdiction (counties)
St Asaph	Denbighshire, Flintshire and Merionethshire
Bangor	Anglesey and Caernarfonshire
Carmarthen	Cardiganshire, Carmarthenshire, Pembrokeshire, and part of Glamorganshire (Gower)
Llandaff	Monmouthshire and Glamorganshire (except Gower)
Hereford	Breconshire, Radnorshire and Herefordshire

The post-1858 records consist of large bound volumes of copy wills that span the years from 1858 until 1941, when registries ceased to copy wills into registers. They cover all the historic counties of Wales (except for Montgomeryshire), and one English county – Herefordshire. Post-1858 Montgomeryshire wills were proved at the Shrewsbury District Registry, the records of which are held at the Shropshire Record Office.

Contemporary manuscript indexes, together with modern card indexes, cover most of the records. Deficiencies can be made up by using the printed *Calendar of Grants*, an annual index of all wills and administrations granted in England and Wales since 1858. This index is available at the Principal Registry of the Family Division, most district probate registries, some local county archive offices and at the National Library of Wales. The availability of this index in Wales is as follows: the Probate Registry of Wales in Cardiff holds a microfiche index for 1973–95 and calendar books for 1956–72; Sub-registries in Bangor and Carmarthen holds a microfiche index for 1973–75, whilst the National Library of Wales holds calendar books for 1858–1972. The amount of records held in Welsh county archives varies from office to office. A brief summary of the holdings for each registry is given below.

St Asaph	Register copy wills, 1858–1928. There are no separate Ms indexes, but indexes can be found in the volumes for 1860–1 and 1865–1923
Bangor	Register copy wills, 1858–1941. Card index, 1858–1941
Carmarthen	Register copy wills, 1858–1941. Ms indexes, 1858–1923. Card index, 1924–41
Llandaff	Register copy wills, 1858–1940. Ms indexes, 1858–1905
Hereford	Register copy wills, 1858–1928. Ms indexes, 1858–1928

In addition to the official probate records, some wills, inventories and other papers associated with probate can be found in the consistory court papers, which are filed with the diocesan records of the Church in Wales. The index to these records can be accessed through the online catalogue of the National Library of Wales.

Hundreds of wills are included in the collections of family, estate and personal papers at Welsh county archive offices and at the National Library of Wales; they can be searched on the latter's online catalogues or through the Archives Wales website. Some of these might not survive in the official probate records or may never have been proved, or might have been proved outside of Wales, but they can also be searched for in the online catalogue of the National Library of Wales.

There are roughly 190,000 wills held at the National Library of Wales and only about 1,000 of these have been written in Welsh, over three quarters of which are from the diocese of Bangor. To give some indication as to the variety of information that can be gleaned from a will, here are a few examples. Amongst the collection are wills of the famous, such as the Welsh Robin Hood, Twm Sion Cati (alias Thomas Johnes), of Fountaine Gate, Caron (SD1609-20); that of Howell Harris, the famous Welsh religious reformer (BR1773-51); and details of a philanderer, namely Oakley Leigh of Lampeter (SD1788-80) who was 'Agent to the tyrannical Squire, Sir Herbert Lloyd.' The parish register recorded his extramarital exploits and no less than eleven 'natural' children were named as beneficiaries in his will. Miles Bassett of Cardiff (LL1680-10) gives details of a family disagreement!

> And [I could put] as little confidence in my crabbed churlish unnaturall, heathenish and unhuman sonne inlaw Leyson Evans and Anne his wife; I never found noe love, shame nor honestie with them … but basenesse and falsehood, knaverie and deceipt in them all, ever unto me … they were my greatest Enemies, I had no comfort in anie of them, but trouble & sorrow ever, they sued me in Londone in the Exchequier and in the Comonpleas, and in the Marches at Ludlowe, and in the great Sessions at Cardiff and thus they have vexed me ever of a long time.

Therefore, a lot of interesting information can be found in wills – information that one would never suspect or may never have found otherwise. They also give an insight into the social conditions, family life and much more. Wills and inventories are an invaluable source for family historians and should not be overlooked.

Further reading
Gibson, Jeremy and Churchill, Else, *Probate Jurisdictions: Where to Look for Wills* (5th edn, FFHS, 2002)
Grannum, Karen and Taylor, Nigel, *Wills and other Probate Records* (TNA, 2004)
Heritage, Celia, *Tracing Your Ancestors through Death Records* (Pen & Sword, 2013)
Raymond, Stuart, A., *The Wills of Our Ancestors* (Pen & Sword, 2012)

Websites

Archives Wales **www.archiveswales.org.uk**

Herefordshire Record Office **www.herefordshire.gov.uk/archives**

Institute of Heraldic and Genealogical Studies **www.ihgs.ac.uk**

National Library of Wales Wills Index **www.llgc.org.uk/probate**

National Library of Wales Online Catalogue **http://cat.llgc.org.uk**

Shropshire Archives **www.shropshire.gov.uk/archives/**

The National Archives
www.nationalarchives.gov.uk/documentsonline/

Chapter 10

MAPS

The use of maps by family historians has increased significantly in recent years because researchers want more information about the locality in which their ancestors lived. There are several types of maps that can add information to what has already been found in parish registers, census returns and other sources.

The National Library of Wales and county archive offices hold large collections of estate records from all across Wales. Amongst these records are manuscript estate maps, which are an invaluable source for plotting the landscape changes that took place in Wales before the introduction of Ordnance Surveys. As these maps are associated with estates it is possible that other, associated documents have survived, such as surveys and rental records that name family members and their connection with the estate.

Towards the end of the nineteenth century, some of these large estates were broken up when tenements were sold at auction. As a result, maps, plans and sale catalogues were created. Many of these found their way to county archive offices and the National Library of Wales and it is worth searching for such sources on their catalogues. In addition, these auctions and sales were frequently recorded in local newspapers that listed buyers and prices paid. For example, the following extract is from a report of the sale of Glynafon Estate, near Llanbeblig; it was found in the *North Wales Express*, 12 September 1870 by using the Welsh newspapers website:

> This valuable freehold estate, situated in the parish of Llanbeblig … The spacious coffee-room was thronged and scores of persons were obliged to remain outside … Appended are the lots with the purchaser's names and price realised:-
> Lot 1, containing Glynafon mansion and plantation, mill, Parc

y Ty, &c, (43 acres 2 roods 19 perches), Mr William Williams, Llanllyfni, £3500.

Lot 2, – Cae Glas, &c, 8a3r 37p, Mr Pierce Williams, Waenfawr £760.

Lot 3, – Part of Glynafon, containing Cae'rbont, and part of Weirglodd y Bont, &c, 6a 2r 2p, Mr Pierce Williams, £480.

Lot 4 , 2 roods 2 perches, Mr Owen Owens, Waenfawr, £80; Lot 5, 12 perches, Mr J. Davies, Llandudno, £42; Lots 6 to 13 were withdrawn, the amount offered being £362; Lot 14, 8 perches, Mr Morris Jones, Post Office, Waenfawr, £71; Lot 15, 26¼ perches, Mr Evan Evans, draper, Waenfawr, £50; Lots 16 to 19 withdrawn, £1807.

Lot 20 – Cae Glas, cottage, &c., 27 perches, Mr Pierce Williams, Waenfawr, £120.

Lot 21 – Part of Tanywaen, containing Cae Bengron, plantation, &c, 4a 3r 36p, Mr Hugh Jones, Brynhelen, £3807.

Lot 22 – Another part of Tanywaen, comprising Cae Berllan, part of Cae'r Ysgol, plantation, &c, 5a 3r 12p, Mr Richard Williams, Penybryn, £400.

Another group of maps are the tithe maps and apportionments. Tithes had been paid by local landowners for the upkeep of the Church and its clergy since the Middle Ages. A tithe was a payment in kind that was equivalent to one tenth of annual produce and was settled with young stock, crops, wool or milk. By the beginning of the nineteenth century it became evident that the tithe should be paid with money, hence the introduction of the Tithe Commutation Act of 1836.

In order to decide on the monetary value of farmland, detailed maps of each farm, which would show the acreage of each field, needed to be drawn. Surveyors were appointed to visit each district in order to map the area and to complete a tithe apportionment to accompany each map.

The original enquiry files for 1,132 districts in Wales are held at The National Archives, Kew. Forty-one of them relate to districts where no tithe was payable and they can be found in TNA Class

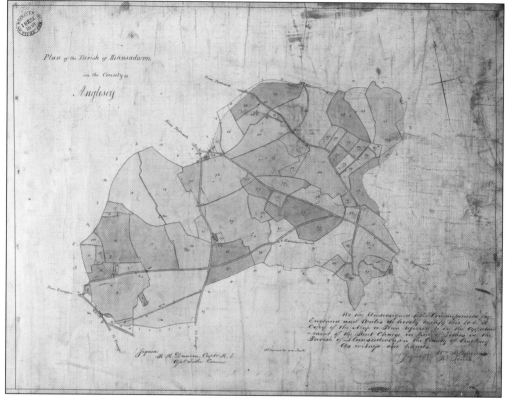

The tithe map of Llansadwrn parish, Anglesey. (NLW)

IR18. Three copies of each map were created, the originals of which are now held at TNA in Class IR 30, whilst the apportionments are held in Class IR 29. The second copy was kept in the parish chest and many of these have now found their way to the county archive offices. The third copy was held by the diocesan registry, of which there were four in Wales, namely: Bangor, St Asaph, St David's and Llandaff. After the disestablishment of the Church in Wales they were transferred to the Welsh Church Commission and are now deposited at the National Library of Wales.

Owing to the magnitude and condition of the maps, the library has made manageable photocopies of each parish tithe map and the accompanying apportionment. These are available on open access in the South Reading Room at the National Library.

On each map, the fields or parcels of land are all numbered; therefore, the apportionment acts as a key to the map. It details the name of the landowner; the occupier; the corresponding number on the plan; the name and description of lands and premises; the quantities of statute measure; and the amount of tithe payable. Some apportionments give field names and the use made of the land, which could be pasture, meadow or arable. The following example is for Little Penpont farm, Llanspyddid parish, Breconshire. The landowner and occupier was Penry Williams.

	Name of land and premises	State of cultivation	Statute A	Measure R	P
40	Cae Passage	Pasture	12	2	16
41	Cae Rallt	Pasture	3	3	15
42	Dwyer	Arable	5	0	13
43	Cae Pan Draw	Arable	5	0	32
44	Cae Pant	Arable	4	3	8
45	Cae Main	Arable	4	2	25
46	Cae Vedw	Pasture	3	2	19
47	Cae Warty	Pasture	1	3	7
48	Shrubbery	Plantation	0	1	16
49	House, Building		0	3	35
50	Wain lass	Meadow	5	1	14
51	Cae Aberon	Arable	4	1	20
52	Waindanty	Meadow	8	0	16
53	Wain hunt	Pasture	1	0	10
54	Wain hunt fawr	Arable	4	2	25
			66	1	11

Tithe maps and apportionments are a very important source of information as they were the most detailed maps produced prior to the introduction of detailed Ordnance Survey maps towards the latter part of the nineteenth century. A digitization project funded by the Heritage Lottery Fund (HLF), led by the Archives and Records Council Wales (ARCW) and entitled 'Cynefin: Mapping Wales' Sense of Place', started in January 2014. The project has digitized and web-mounted the 1,110 tithe maps for Wales held at the National Library of Wales (see list of websites at the end of the chapter). They have been geo-referenced and the accompanying apportionments have been transcribed by online volunteers.

We have all used Ordnance Survey (OS) maps at some point in our lives, possibly to find a village or property associated with our ancestors. The OS is the national mapping authority for Great Britain and in 1801 its map of Kent was the first to use a scale of 1 inch to a mile. The National Library of Wales holds an almost complete collection of OS maps, in all scales, for Wales. These include original surveyors' drawings, for the period between 1809 and 1840, at the scale of 2 inches to a mile. These were later used to draw maps of Wales, on a scale of 1-inch to a mile, from 1818 to 1842.

The more detailed 6-inch and 25-inch county series of maps were not produced until the 1860s; various editions appeared thereafter and metric equivalents were published from the 1950s onwards. In recent years, Ordnance Survey maps have been produced digitally and they are all available to view in the South Reading Room of the National Library of Wales. Most county archive offices also hold relevant maps for their own counties.

These maps can be used in conjunction with other maps and sources in order to locate where your ancestors lived, to understand the land in that area, especially if it is in a rural locality, and to show the development of urban areas. Names of properties may have changed over the years and buildings will have changed shape and use: OS maps also show these developments and can be used alongside other records to document such changes. Many of the historical OS maps are reproduced by commercial companies such as Cassini Maps and Alan Godfrey maps and are available in digital or paper format. Further information can also be found on the Ordnance Survey website.

The Valuation Office survey was a result of the 1910 Finance Act and is often known as the Lloyd George 'Domesday'. The survey produced printed OS maps that were annotated by hand and field books that provided additional information about a property. The plans and field books are held at TNA; plans for Wales can be found in Class IR 131/1-11. To determine the plan for your area, use the online Valuation Office map finder and online research guides of TNA. County archive offices and the National Library of Wales also hold stray copies of plans and field books.

Also held at TNA are the National Farm Surveys taken during the Second World War, which give detailed information that relates to all farms and smallholdings of 5 acres and above in England and Wales. Individual farm records can be found in Class MAF 32; these are arranged by county, then alphabetically by parish within the county. These records comprise four forms that show:

- details of small fruit, vegetables, stocks of hay and straw;
- details in respect of agricultural land;
- the Farm Survey;
- labour, motive power, rent and length of occupancy.

Further details relating to both the Valuation Office surveys and the National Farm Survey can be found in online research guides on the TNA website

Further reading
Beech, Geraldine and Mitchell, Rose, *Maps for Family and Local Historians* (TNA, 2004)
Davies, Robert, *The Tithe Maps of Wales, a Guide to the Tithe Maps in the National Library of Wales* (NLW, 1997)
Kain, Roger J. P. and Prince, Hugh C., *Tithe Surveys for Historians* (Phillimore, 2000)
Masters, Charles, *Essential Maps For Family Historians* (Countryside Books, 2009)

Websites
Alan Godfrey Maps **www.alangodfreymaps.co.uk/**
Cassini Maps **www.cassinimaps.co.uk/**

Cynefin: The Tithe Maps of Wales
www.cynefin.archiveswales.org.uk/
National Library of Wales Guide to Maps
www.llgc.org.uk/collections/learn-more/introduction3/
Ordnance Survey **www.ordnancesurvey.co.uk**
The National Archives Research Guides
www.nationalarchives.gov.uk/records/atoz/
The National Archives Valuation Office Map Finder
www.labs.nationalarchives.gov.uk/wordpress/index.php/201
/04/valuation-office-map-finder/

Chapter 11

NEWSPAPERS

It was not until 28 January 1804 that the first newspaper in Wales was published. This was *The Cambrian*, an English-language weekly newspaper published in Swansea. It included local and national news, advertisements and notices. The newspaper ran until March 1930 when it was merged with other newspapers to become *The Herald of Wales*. Swansea Library service has created an online index known as The Cambrian Indexing Project, which contains thousands of entries. The index includes all reported births, marriages and deaths, and articles are arranged by topic: transport, ships and shipping, disasters and accidents, planning and land management, buildings, agriculture, industry, education, health and welfare, religion, politics, crime, culture, sport, and uniformed forces. The resource is used extensively by those with connections in the Swansea, Neath and Port Talbot areas, but also includes entries from further afield. Remember that it is only an index and does not show the articles themselves; however, it is a helpful tool when used in conjunction with Welsh Newspapers Online, which is referred to later.

North Wales soon followed with its first weekly, *The North Wales Gazette*, which was first published in 1808 and later became *The North Wales Chronicle*. *The Caernarvon Herald* began in 1830 and later appeared as *The Caernarvon and Denbigh Herald*, which covered most of north Wales. There was some conflict between the two papers as *The Herald* was Liberal and nonconformist, whilst *The Chronicle* had a Tory and Established Church bias. *The Carmarthen Journal*, which covered west Wales, was first published in 1810 and was a Conservative paper; *The Carmarthen Journal* and *The North Wales Chronicle* are still published today.

Early newspapers consisted of few pages and one page was

Front page of The Cambrian, *which was the earliest newspaper in Wales (NLW)*

usually dedicated to adverts, which provided a source of income. National and international news was included but usually this was copied from London papers such as the *London Gazette*. The first Welsh language weekly to be published was *Seren Gomer* (The Star of Gomer) founded by Joseph Harris 'Gomer' in 1814. Its aims were to publish the following news:

- Home
- Foreign
- Political
- Religious
- Literary contributions that would safeguard and spread the Welsh language

Unlike the English language weeklies, which published mainly local news, *Seren Gomer* was a national newspaper for the whole of Wales. It had a large circulation, but came to an end after only eighty-five issues; this was mainly due to the tax on paper, which made it too expensive, and the income generated from adverts, which was too small.

The first daily newspapers published in Wales were national newspapers that provided home and national news and placed importance on political and social issues. The first in Wales was *The Cambria Daily Leader*, a Liberal paper, which was established in Swansea, in 1861. *The South Wales Daily News* was established in Cardiff in 1872 and *The South Wales Daily Post* in Swansea in 1893. By far the most popular daily paper is *The Western Mail,* which continues to be published today and was established, in 1869, as a Conservative newspaper that promoted the political aims of the Marquis of Bute.

James Rees of Caernarfon was probably the most important newspaper publisher in north Wales. In 1855, he established *Yr Herald Cymraeg*, a Liberal newspaper with a large circulation in the counties of Anglesey and Caernarfonshire. Literature featured prominently in its columns and it employed some of the most prominent writers of the time, such as Llew Llwyfo, Richard Hughes Williams and T. Gwynn Jones. Caernarfon was also the birthplace of

Y Genedl Gymreig (The Welsh Nation) in 1877. It was an influential newspaper and was bought by a group of MPs, including David Lloyd George, in 1892. In that year Beriah Gwynfe Evans became its editor and *Y Genedl* developed into a national newspaper with a special south Wales edition.

Aberdare and Merthyr Tydfil, both in the heart of the south Wales coalfield, developed as important centres for newspaper publishing. *The Aberdare Times* was established in 1861, but the most important of all the papers was *Tarian y Gweithiwr*, which ran from 1875 to 1934 and was a Liberal–Labour weekly. It appealed mainly to the miners and tin workers of south Wales and provided a mixture of local and national news.

Not far from Aberdare, Merthyr Tydfil had several newspapers of its own. *The Cardiff and Merthyr Guardian*, *The Merthyr Star* and *Y Fellten*. In 1873, *The Workman's Advocate/Amddiffynydd y Gweithiwr* was established; it was a bilingual radical newspaper that continued the tradition begun by *Y Gweithiwr* and *Udgorn Cymru*, which were published in the town between 1834 and 1840 and were associated with the Chartist movement.

Towns all over Wales also had their own newspapers, even the smaller market towns of Brecon, Newcastle Emlyn, Pwllheli and Aberystwyth. The number of newspapers published in Wales increased considerably when the tax on advertisements and the stamp duty on newspaper copies were abolished in 1854 and 1865 respectively. Many denominational newspapers were also established after this period.

By the late 1880s, over seventy-nine English weekly papers and twenty-five Welsh weekly papers were being published in Wales, a level of activity which caused J.E. Vincent to remark in the *London Times* in 1889:

> The growth of journalism and of vernacular journalism in particular, in the Principality has of late years been little short of phenomenal. My impression, indeed, is that Wales supports more journals in proportion to its population than any other part of the civilised world.

Welsh Newspapers Online is a free resource from the National Library of Wales. It will allow anyone with an interest in Wales and the Welsh to browse and search over 100 titles from the newspapers that were produced before 1910. Not only can digital pages be searched and viewed when using Welsh Newspapers Online, but optical character recognition technology allows the researcher to look for words, names and dates simultaneously within the one million pages of this resource. This adds significant value to the collection because it allows researchers to discover countless nuggets of genealogical information that would otherwise remain hidden within the covers of the heavy bound volumes in Aberystwyth.

For family historians, a good place to start is a search of birth, marriage and death notices; 'ordinary' people were included from about the mid-nineteenth century. Notices may also give you more biographical information than conventional certificates or parish register entries: as in the case of these three marriage notices from the *Cardiff Times*, 2 July 1881, which are all connected by a double wedding and the marriage of twins:

> On June 30 at Adamsdown Meeting Room, Cardiff, William Akers of Cardiff to Mary Annie, eldest daughter of Thomas Baker, Wyndcliffe House, Roath

> On June 30 at Adamsdown Meeting Room, Cardiff, Harry Godfrey of Teignmouth to Emily, second daughter of the above-named Thomas Baker

> On June 27 at Teighnmouth, Charles Donges of London to Annie Godfrey twin sister of the above-named Harry Godfrey

Marriage reports towards the end of the nineteenth century often reveal all sorts of details, as they would list wedding guests and wedding presents, and provide detailed accounts of outfits worn and the proceedings of the day. During the twentieth century it was also common to include wedding photographs in the paper.

Death notices, obituaries and details of wills are all an invaluable source for any family historian. Notices will possibly give you details of where someone was buried, which could lead to you visiting the graveyard or searching for monumental inscriptions that have been transcribed by a family history society. Obituaries can vary in length and detail but, during the twentieth century, it was common to include some background information about the deceased, the names of attendees at the funeral and their relationship to deceased, along with an account of the service. Details of wills often include information that would not necessarily be found in the *Calendar of Grants*, as in the case of 'Shani Pob Man' (alias Jane Leonard) from the *Welsh Gazette*, 12 April 1917:

> Shani Pob Man, a queer old character residing near New Quay, had died and left a will properly executed. A sum of £104 16s 4½d was found in the house and she had left all her property to Aberayron Hospital . . . The Clerk added that there were 1,000 three-penny bits and two drawers full of coppers. The sack weighted 56lbs … the woman was a native of Mydroilyn and had been an inmate of the Workhouse. She had received small coins from visitors. She had acted quite honourably and had repaid all that was due to the Union.

If a death was the result of an accident or tragedy, an inquest would have been held and detailed reports tended to appear in the newspaper. Such reports are an invaluable resource, especially if the original coroner's records for the death you are researching are no longer available. Newspapers are crucial when tracing information on local and national events: from an industrial accident to a local tragedy. You may also find an ancestor amongst the numerous reports of eisteddfodau (a Welsh festival of literature, music and performance) or local agricultural shows and events throughout Wales.

Quarter and Petty Sessions were also reported in detail: especially useful if you had not considered this source previously or you have discovered that the original records for the area in question are not available. Whether an ancestor broke the law, was a victim of crime, or was mentioned in a newspaper for any other reason, being able to search Welsh Newspapers Online by name or date is invaluable.

It must be remembered that this resource is not a complete collection of Welsh newspapers, but the National Library of Wales, regional archive offices and public libraries hold extensive collections of newspapers in original and microfilm format. Therefore, if you are unable to find a title or date on Welsh Newspapers Online, enquire to see what is held elsewhere. The British Library website, The British Newspaper Archive, also has a vast collection online, including several Welsh titles that often extend further than 1910 and can be searched online through Findmypast. A search can be made for free but a charge is made for viewing the digital images. It must also be remembered that Welsh people would have been mentioned in newspapers much further afield than those published in Wales, so all sources are worth checking for information.

Further reading
Jones, Beti, *Newsplan: Report of the NEWSPLAN Project in Wales: adroddiad ar gynllun NEWSPLAN yng Nghymru* (Aberystwyth, 1993)

Websites
British Newspaper Archive **www.britishnewspaperarchive.co.uk**
The Cambrian Indexing Project, Swansea Library Service
www.swansea.gov.uk/index.cfm?articleid=8465
Findmypast **www.findmypast.co.uk**
The National Library of Wales **www.llgc.org.uk**
Welsh Newspapers Online **www.welshnewspapers.llgc.org.uk**

Chapter 12

THE POOR LAW AFTER 1834

An increase in poverty throughout England and Wales during the early part of the nineteenth century meant that the old Poor Law system became ineffective. As a result, 'An Act for the Amendment and better Administration of the Laws relating to the Poor in England and Wales' was introduced – better known as the Poor Law Amendment Act of 1834. The new system was to replace the old one by concentrating on the 'indoor relief' provided by workhouses rather than the 'outdoor relief' provided by home visits from the parish officers.

The first task of the Poor Law commissioners was to unite parishes in order to create 'unions': forty-seven were originally created in Wales. Each union was required to have its own workhouse to house paupers; but by 1845, only thirty of the Welsh unions had a building that was suitable to be used as a workhouse. By 1860 there were still six unions without an adequate workhouse, but further pressure from the Poor Law commissioners saw them comply. In 1879, Rhayader was the last union to open its new workhouse. A list of unions for Wales, with date of creation, appears in Appendix 8.

The newly created Poor Law unions were run by boards of guardians. The guardians were elected annually by the ratepayers and the number of guardians per union was decided by the commissioners. The board met regularly – every week at first, and later every fortnight – and reported to the Poor Law Commission in London. Their responsibilities included the administration of births, marriages and deaths; vaccinations and other public health issues; and indoor and outdoor relief. They also appointed staff to help them in this work: workhouse masters and matrons, relieving officers, clerks, treasurers, medical officers, schoolmasters and chaplains.

Workhouses were intentionally uncomfortable to live in so that

ABERAYRON UNION.

PAROCHIAL LIST OF OUT-DOOR POOR for the Half-Year ending September, 1866.

Remarks	Names of the Paupers	Where Resident	No. of Parishes	Cause of requiring Relief	Amount

Remarks	Names of the Paupers	Where Resident	No. of Parishes	Cause of requiring Relief	£ s. d.

NUMBERS REFERRED TO.

CILCENNIN	1	LLANDDEWI — 12
CILIEAYRON	2	LLANEBCHAYRON — 11
HENFYNYW	5	LLANSANTFFREAD — 9
LLANBADARN	7	YSTRAD — 14

D. JONES,

Relieving Officer.

List of 'out-door' relief paupers in the Aberayron Union, 1866. (NLW, Poster C13)

those able to work and fend for themselves were encouraged to do so without relief. The new system did meet with some opposition and a few workhouses were targeted by protesters. However, the protesters against the new Poor Law argued that many seeking help were victims of unemployment and low pay, and needed assistance whilst they tried to gain employment. Narberth, Carmarthen, Llanfyllin, and Newtown and Llanidloes union workhouses all became targets of the 'Rebecca Rioters', who protested against the cost of forming the workhouses, especially in the poor rural areas of Wales.

Admission to the workhouse was managed by the relieving officer or workhouse master, but overseen by the board of guardians. It would have been a last resort for most inmates. Men, women and children were separated, as were the able-bodied and those who were disabled. Workhouse inmates would sleep in large dormitories, or wards, in segregated wings of the workhouse. A strict daily routine of eating, working and sleeping was followed. The conditions in workhouses throughout Wales varied, but, during the first half of the nineteenth century, they acquired a reputation for being harsh, cruel and demeaning places.

Segregation rules of Paupers from the Poor Law
Commissioners Report

The in-door paupers shall be classed as follows-
1. Aged or infirm men
2. Able-bodied men and youths above 13
3. Youths and boys above seven years old and under 13
4. Aged or infirm women
5. Able-bodied women and girls above 16
6. Girls above seven years of age and under 16
7. Children under seven years of age
To each class shall be assigned by the board of guardians that apartment or separate building which may be best fitted for the section of such class, and in which they shall respectively remain, without communication, unless as is hereinafter provided.

Much of the work of the board of guardians was a continuation of the work carried out by parish officers. Amongst other duties, they pursued matters of settlement and removal; they chased fathers of illegitimate children for maintenance payments; they dealt with maintenance payments for relatives; and they traced men and women who had deserted their families, making them chargeable to the parish. Here is an extract from Machynlleth Poor Law Union minute book (NLW, Henry Evans 1) for 31 July 1839:

Order that the Parish Officers of the undermd Parishes be directed to attend the Petty Sessions and make Complaints against the undermentioned persons who have deserted their families whereby they are become chargeable to the Parishes

Llanbrynmair	Evan Richard	Labrer now at Merthyr	
Do	Thomas Davies	Do	Do
Do	Lewis Williams	Do	Do
Cemmes	John Roberts	Do	Do
Isygarreg	Vaughan Evans	Do	Do
Scyborycoed	John Williams	Tailor	Do
Penegoes	Edward Whittington		
Towyn	David Hughes	Laborer	Do
Do	Richard David	Do	Do
Do	Evan Jones	Shoemaker	Do
Do	John Francis	Laborer	supposed to be about Chester or Carnarvon
Llanwrin	Hugh Lewis	Weaver	Llanidloes

Towards the end of the nineteenth century, conditions improved slightly when unions found that providing 'outdoor' relief was cheaper and better than life in the workhouse. As a result, there was a decline in the use of workhouses and many of the buildings were put to other uses at the beginning of the twentieth century, such as mental hospitals, cottage hospitals and children's homes. In 1929, the workhouses were abolished, but the Poor Law unions themselves continued until 1948, when they were replaced by the welfare state and administration was transferred to local governments.

The Poor Law unions received advice from several bodies during their existence:

- Poor Law Commissioners 1834–47
- Poor Law Board 1848–71
- Local Government Board 1871–1919
- Ministry of Health 1919–29

The records relating to the Poor Law unions can be found at The National Archives, Kew and county archive offices; there are also a few items at the National Library of Wales, Aberystwyth. Amongst the records at the National Library of Wales are nine volumes of letter books written between 1836 and 1844 by William Day, who was the assistant Poor Law commissioner for Wales and Shropshire. The volumes, some of which have lists of contents, consist of copies of his reports and copies of his letters to the Poor Law Commission in London, to colleagues, and to the officials of boards of guardians, along with circulars, memoranda, and so on. These documents relate to various Poor Law unions in Wales and to some in England, particularly in Shropshire (NLW, Mss 3141–9F).

The National Archives holds records that relate to the Poor Law commissioners and to the successive advisory committees mentioned above:

- Class MH9 – staff employment records, 1837–1921, arranged by county, then alphabetically by Poor Law union.
- Class MH12 – correspondence, 1834–1900 (later records destroyed by fire), arranged by county, then alphabetically by Poor Law union. Mostly contains correspondence relating to the administration of individual workhouses.
- Class MH14 – plans and drawings of individual workhouses, 1861–1918.
- Class MH32 – records that relate to the reports of inspectors, arranged alphabetically by name of inspector.

The first evidence you may find for ancestors who either had a connection to the workhouse or received relief will be through census returns and parish records. They may appear in the workhouse as inmates or they may be recorded as paupers who lived in the community and received outdoor relief.

A good place to start searching for surviving records is the book by Jeremy Gibson and Colin Rogers, which lists the variety of documentation available and notes the dates for which records exist with regard to the Welsh unions. County archive offices hold an array of records that relate to the Poor Law unions for their respective county, but bear in mind that many unions on county borders were formed from parishes that were located in two or more counties; therefore, checking holdings in all relevant county archive offices is a must. The Archives Wales website is also a good place to search, in case other records have come to light since the publication of the book. There are also records held at the National Library of Wales that can be searched through the Archives Wales site or directly through its online catalogue.

Newspapers are also a great source for the minutes of meetings of boards of guardians and can give detailed accounts, which is especially useful when no other records have survived. Local newspapers also recorded events at the workhouses, such as unexpected deaths, tea parties, Christmas dinners, reports on living conditions and the state of the buildings.

For a more in-depth understanding of the workhouse system and what life was like for workhouse inmates, Peter Higginbotham's website is an essential source of information, along with his various publications on the topic.

Further reading

Cole, Anne, *An Introduction to Poor Law Documents before 1834* (FFHS, 2000)

Fowler, Simon, *Workhouse: The People, The Places, The Life Behind Doors* (TNA, 2008)

Fowler, Simon, *Poor Law Records for Family Historians* (FHP, 2011)

Gibson, Jeremy and Rogers, Colin, *Poor Law Union Records, Vol. 3 – South West England, the Marches and Wales* (FFHS, 2000)

Websites

Archives Wales **www.archiveswales.org**

Llanfyllin workhouse **www.llanfyllinworkhouse.org**

Peter Higginbotham Workhouses **www.workhouses.org.uk**

Powys Archives www.a-day-in-the-life.powys.org.uk/eng/ social/es_compare.php

The National Library of Wales **www.cat.llgc.org.uk**

Welsh Newspapers Online **www.welshnewspapers.llgc.org.uk**

West Glamorgan Archive Service **www.swansea.gov.uk/westglamorganarchives**

Chapter 13

EDUCATION

It is well documented that the provision of education in England and Wales before the second half of the nineteenth century was completely inadequate. At the beginning of the century elementary education for children of the working classes depended on the voluntary efforts of the Church of England, Sunday schools of various denominations, charitable societies and private schools known as dame schools and private adventure schools.

Many grammar schools were founded in Wales during the sixteenth and seventeenth centuries, the earliest being Christ College Brecon in 1541. However, the early registers and pupil records for those who attended have not survived, unlike those for English grammar schools. In fact, few sources have survived from before the end of the eighteenth century. One of the earliest documents is the Beaumaris School Roll, 1785–1869 (David Hughes Charity Mss) held at Anglesey Archives. Records of other grammar schools may be held at the National Library of Wales or county archive offices and a search of the Archives Wales website will assist in tracing any records that can be accessed at Welsh repositories.

As Wales did not have its own university at this time, many of the Welsh went to the universities of Oxford and Cambridge. *Alumni Oxoniensis* and *Alumni Cantabrigiensis* contain details of attendees at the universities until the end of the nineteenth century: many of them were Welshmen. Details shown can include parentage, along with place and year of birth; additionally, the student's academic career and subsequent achievements are often given. Jesus College, Oxford, has for some time been known as 'The Welsh College'; between 1571 and 1915 it saw no less than twenty-four principals from Wales or of Welsh descent. By 1600, almost all of its students were Welsh and came from a wide spectrum of backgrounds: sons of farm workers, labourers and miners to landed gentry and nobility. There continues to be a strong connection between the college and Wales, but more restrictions have been put in place over the years.

The nonconformists were not allowed to attend the Anglican grammar schools and English universities; therefore, they established numerous nonconformist academies in Wales. The first of these was Brynllywarch, Glamorgan, which opened in 1662 and was followed in subsequent centuries by numerous private academies and theological colleges run by various denominations, the main ones being in Carmarthen, Brecon, Trefeca and Bala. Papers relating to various nonconformist academies and colleges are kept at the National Library of Wales.

One of the main events in the history of education prior to 1800 was the founding of the Welsh Trust schools by Thomas Gouge in 1674. These schools were later followed by the Society for the Promotion of Christian Knowledge (SPCK), which was established in 1699; the chief aim of the SPCK was 'to set up Charity schools for teaching poor children to read and write and to repeat and understand the Church Catechism'. The Society established ninety-six schools in Wales before 1740, mostly in the counties of Pembrokeshire, Glamorganshire and Carmarthenshire. Although it began as an interdenominational body, the SPCK soon became specifically Anglican.

In September 1731, Griffith Jones of Llanddowror wrote to the SPCK proposing a 'Welch School' at Llanddowror. He had been a member of the society since 1713 and had previously worked as a teacher in the society's school at Laugharne. Sometime during the 1730s (there is no accurate date), the circulating Welsh charity schools were established by Griffith Jones and were fully operational by 1737. These schools were held in whatever buildings were available – very often in parish churches. The Bible and catechism were the textbooks. Unlike his predecessors, Griffith Jones was not concerned about literacy 'but for the salvation of soul; literacy by enabling believers to study God's word'. A school session would last three or four months and classes were usually held during the daytime, although there is later evidence of occasional night schools.

Our knowledge of the development and contribution of Griffith Jones' schools can be attributed to the publication of an annual report, *Welch Piety*, which survives in an unbroken run from 1738 to 1777. *Welch Piety* included reports from parishes and lists of the previous year's schools held in each area, along with the number of students in attendance. Copies can be viewed at the National Library of Wales.

Griffith Jones died in 1761, he bequeathed the funds of the schools and his own private money – which totalled £7,000 – to Bridget Bevan, so that she could continue with the good work of the schools; she did this very successfully until her death in 1779. Sadly, after her death, the £10,000 sum that she bequeathed in order for the schools to be continued was locked in Chancery for thirty years, until 1804. By this time it had cumulated into more than £30,000 and was reallocated to the circulating schools. However, by the 1850s, the changes in the educational system, and the fact that the funds had been held in Chancery for so long, contributed to the end of the movement.

During the eighteenth century, many charitable endowments were made in order to educate the poor in England and Wales: *The Digest of Schools and Charities* (1842) lists seventy-nine such endowments in Wales. The Sunday schools and circulating schools had played a significant part in the educational history of Wales. However, the growing population, and the enthusiasm of the people for becoming better educated and improving themselves, meant that the educational needs of the early nineteenth century called for new types of schools to be established.

The National Society for Promoting the Education of the Poor in the Principles of the Established Church (The National Society) was established in 1811, to support the work of the parish schools. The key aims of The National Society were: to teach basic literacy skills, usually by reading the Bible, and the basics of arithmetic; its second aim was to improve morals and conduct; and third, it sought to train girls for employment as servants and housekeepers, as well as for their roles as wives and mothers. The society believed that if they worked fast enough to educate the children of the poor, who were

Rules & Regulations

OF THE

MONMOUTH

NATIONAL SCHOOLS

1.—The hours of attendance at the School are, from Lady-day to Michaelmas, Nine to Twelve in the Morning, and Two to Half-past Four in the Afternoon. From Michaelmas to Lady-day, Nine to Twelve in the Morning, and Two to Four in the Afternoon.

2.—No School on Saturdays.

On every Sunday, School at Half-past Nine in the Morning, and Half-past Two in the Afternoon.

RULES.

1.—That every Child be sent to School regularly at the above-mentioned Hours, and that no Child, on any account, be absent from School without first obtaining leave of the proper authorities.

2.—That every Child be sent to School with clean Hands and Face, Hair kept cut, and Clothes neatly mended.

3.—That Parents wishing to take their Children from School shall give notice to the Committee beforehand.

4.—That every Child shall attend School on Sundays, both Morning and Afternoon, and also Divine Service.

5.—That every Child instructed in the above Schools be required to pay Two Pence per week; for two Children belonging to the same family, Three Pence; and for any number exceeding two, Four Pence per Week, in each School. Payment to be made on the day of admission, and every Monday Morning afterwards.

☞ *These Rules and Regulations must be strictly observed by the Children belonging to the above Schools, and by their Parents.*

T. FARROR, PRINTER, MONMOUTH.

Rules and regulations of the Monmouth National Schools. (NLW, Poster XLB)

a large percentage of the country's youngsters, they would gain a majority over the nonconformists within a generation.

The main drawback of the early national schools in Wales was that the children were mainly monoglot Welsh-speakers: very few understood, let alone used, the English language – unlike their teachers. As no speaking was allowed in the classrooms under National Society rules, children were unable to use or gain further understanding of English, so when they were reading they had no concept of the meanings of the words in their books. The syllabus was limited to the three Rs, although SPCK did provide books and apparatus. Many were critical of the system, but at the beginning of the nineteenth century it was the only way that thousands of children could gain any education and hope for the future.

In 1801, Joseph Lancaster, a Quaker, introduced a similar teaching system to The National Society's. However, the only religious textbook was be the Bible. The curriculum concentrated on reading, writing and arithmetic taught by rote and non-denominational religious instruction. The National Society's system of teaching was unacceptable to the nonconformists and 1814 saw the formation of the British and Foreign Schools Society (the British Society).

Religion was one of the most powerful influences on determining the pattern of education in Wales. The church believed that it was their duty to take care of the moral and spiritual development of the people. The growth of nonconformity and especially the differences between the Calvinistic Methodists and the Established Church played a prominent part in Welsh education.

By the mid-nineteenth century many weaknesses in the provision of education had been highlighted. But the strength of Sunday schools and the few day schools, as well as the increased involvement of the British Society in accepting government funding to build elementary schools, gave hope 'to the whole of Wales' (according to the British Society); it was hoped that in future, better school provision, improved facilities and a greater number of trained teachers would be available. The desire to be educated increased, along with a rapid growth in British schools, which saw the commencement of a new era in elementary education in Wales. Sunday schools played an important role in the lives of the Welsh people during the nineteenth century, as they helped to create a population of adults and children who were literate in their native Welsh.

State intervention in education in England and Wales increased after 1839 with the establishment of the Committee of the Council on Education. Its objectives were to oversee the spending of government grants for promoting public education in both countries.

School pupils of Pencarreg school, Carmarthenshire, 1891. (NLW, John Thomas Collection)

To qualify for a grant, the local community would have to raise some of its own money. Because large parts of Wales were poverty stricken, the number of requests for assistance in building schools in Wales during the 1830s and 1840s was minimal.

The first HMIs, John Allen and Hugh Tremenheere, found that there was growing concern for the state of education in England and Wales prior to their 1847 Report. Tremenheere reported on the mining districts of south Wales and found few British Society schools in the area. Sir Hugh Owen, a founder of the British Society in Wales, recognized that the nonconformist voluntaryists would be unable to provide adequate education for the children without government support. Therefore, in his public letter 'to the Welsh People' in 1843, he urged the people of Wales to accept these grants, which later contributed to the pressure put on the government to conduct an enquiry into the state of education in Wales.

The commissioners who had in 1844 inquired into the disturbances of the Rebecca Riots, attributed them partly to a lack of education and particularly to the labouring classes' lack of knowledge of the English language, which caused difficulties in establishing law and order. William Williams, a Welshman and MP for Coventry, argued that education in Wales had been insufficiently discussed – particularly since the language problem complicated matters. By 1846, following many months of discussion, the government agreed to set up a Commission to Inquire into the State of Education in Wales. The commissioners were instructed to examine the capacity of the classrooms; the state of the furniture; the numbers of children on the registers; average attendance; organization and methods used; whether instruction was given in Welsh or English; and the number of teachers, as well as their ages and training. In 1847, the Reports of the Commissioners of Inquiry into the State of Education in Wales – 'The Blue Books' – were published. These were detailed and thorough reports, which strongly attacked the standard of education, the competence of the teachers and the state of school buildings in Wales. The numerous problems and difficulties faced by schools prior to this date were now to be highlighted.

The commissioners were also expected to estimate the general condition and state of intelligence of the poorer classes and how improved education might be expected to influence the general condition of society and its moral and religious process. The classification of schools was made on the basis of whether they were church or non-church.

The main aim of the curricula taught throughout elementary schools in Wales at the time was to educate pupils in English, reading, writing and arithmetic. The syllabuses varied greatly from school to school. Using the English language for instruction created its own problems: it was a great handicap in educational instruction in all subjects because of teachers' ignorance of teaching techniques and the children's inability to understand lessons delivered in English. The teaching of reading was of an unsatisfactory standard because the language and vocabulary of the set reading books was incomprehensible to monoglot Welsh-speaking children.

The use of the 'Welsh Not' or 'Welsh Stick' or 'Welsh Lead' was established as a form of punishment well before the commissioners visited Welsh schools in 1846 and 1847. Many accounts of the various methods adopted to discourage children from speaking Welsh at school are recorded amongst reminiscences and memoirs of Welsh people, the most famous being O. M. Edwards' detailed description of the use in Llanuwchllyn of the Welsh Not system that contributed so much to the degradation of the Welsh language in schools in Wales. The Welsh Not, or W.N., was a small piece of wood on a piece of string if a child was heard speaking Welsh, he/she was compelled to wear the Not around their neck. In the morning it would be given, at random, to one of the children and was passed on to any child overheard speaking Welsh. At the end of the school day, whoever was wearing the Welsh Not would be given a lashing.

In spite of all the controversy associated with the reports, which are commonly known as 'Brad y Llyfrau Gleision – The Treachery of the Blue Books', much of the factual evidence was true and was seen as a step in the right direction for the improvement of the educational system in Wales. However, the facts and opinions presented in the report appear to be biased in favour of an English, generally Anglican, education. The commissioners were often critical of the Welsh language and dissension associated with it; they also over-emphasized certain aspects of the people's moral standards and social habits. As a result, the evidence gathered by the commissioners regarding the poor conditions of school buildings and sanitation, the lack of teaching equipment and the low standards of education, was pushed into the background to some degree, due to the excessive emphasis on the children's inability to communicate in English. Many regarded the report as no less than treachery and thought it had failed to address the true educational needs of Wales. Digital images of all three volumes of 'The Blue Books' can be viewed online through the National Library of Wales website www.llgc.org.uk/index.php?id=thebluebooks

The Education Act of 1870 was a major landmark in the educational history of England and Wales. It marked the commencement of a national system of elementary education provided by state-supported voluntary schools. In areas where there was a deficiency of schools this was administered by a new school board. As a result, regulations saw to it that school reports were kept and admission records, attendance registers and log books were introduced. However, the amount of information shown by these records does vary: the most basic only give the name and address of a pupil, whilst others are more comprehensive and provide a mine of genealogical information such as date of birth, parentage, occupation of father, and dates of admission and withdrawal. Log books were kept daily to record all manner of things that took place at the school. These included visits, absences, illness, punishment, examiners reports, and so on, although the detail of the information given may vary from school to school. From 1876 onwards, it was compulsory for all parents to send their children to school; however, full-time education for those between the ages of 5 and 10 had to wait until the Elementary Education Act was introduced in 1880. The Board of Education Act of 1899 and the Education Act of 1918 raised the school-leaving age to 12 and 14 respectively.

The 1902 Education Act passed control of all board, national and British schools to the county councils. As a result, all the records that related to education should be held at the relevant county record offices; these may include the admissions, progress and withdrawal registers, log books, various account books, daily attendance registers and minute books. Some schools have records that are more complete than those of other schools and whilst some have retained their records, the records of others may have passed into private ownership.

Secondary education was transformed as a result of the Welsh Intermediate Education Act in 1889. The Act created a network of publicly funded, non-denominational secondary schools for boys and girls which were administrated by the local education authorities set up by the county councils. Again, various records that relate to secondary schools are held at the county record offices.

The University of Wales was established as a federal university in 1893 as a result of campaigns by the people of Wales for the right to further education in their own country. It was formed with the foundation colleges of University College Wales (now Aberystwyth University), founded in 1872; University College North Wales (now Bangor University), founded in 1884; and University College South Wales and Monmouthshire (now Cardiff University), founded in 1883. The University at Lampeter was founded in 1822 and is the oldest in Wales to award degrees and the third oldest in England and Wales (after Oxford and Cambridge). In 1971, it became known as St David's University College before joining the University of Wales in 1996 and is now known as University of Wales Trinity St David. The Welsh University colleges of Aberystwyth, Bangor, Cardiff and Trinity St David have their own archive departments or libraries, which house a vast collection of manuscripts and printed sources relating to their history and students. Available records can be searched for through their individual websites or through Archives Wales, as can records for other universities within Wales that may be held by county archive offices or at the National Library of Wales.

Further reading
Elwyn Jones, Gareth, *The Education of a Nation* (UWP, 1997)
Elwyn Jones, Gareth and Wynne Roderick, Gordon, *A History of Education in Wales* (UWP, 2003)

Websites
Archives Wales **www.archiveswales.org.uk**
The National Library of Wales **www.cat.llgc.org.uk**

Chapter 14

ESTATE AND MANORIAL RECORDS

Once you have discovered as much as you can via parish registers, census returns and civil registration records, you may find that the next step in tracing your family back further will be to turn to estate and manorial records. Until the twentieth century, landed estates owned by the gentry were prominent throughout Wales. At some point, most of the population have or worked on these estates. Estate records are very important as they contain information that relates to many aspects of life in Wales. Additionally, these families were often connected with industry, as the natural resources were sourced from their land; they also provided financial help for developments.

Some of the most substantial family and estate archives held at the National Library of Wales include those of the following estates: Badminton; Tredegar; Bute; Powis Castle; Wynnstay; Chirk Castle; and Penrice and Margam; the records reflect the growth, development and influence of these families in Wales over a long period of time.

These collections can include records such as:

- Manorial records
- Title deeds and other documents that relate to the transfer of property
- Rental lists that include names of tenants and details of property
- Correspondence
- Administration documents
- Accounts, including workers' wages

It has been suggested that manorial records are one of the most important groups of genealogical records after parish registers and wills. This group consists of various types of documents and the Manorial Documents Rules of 1959 define these records as:

> court rolls, surveys, maps, terriers, documents and books of every description relating to the boundaries, wastes, customs and courts of a manor.

But what is a manor? Without going into detail, a manor was a piece of land, which could vary greatly in size; the lord of the manor granted land to tenants in return for rent and services. Each manor also had a manor court over which the lord or his steward would preside, whilst the tenants would act as jurors. The courts would set out the conditions of tenure; create by-laws, also known as 'customs of the manor'; appoint minor officials within the manor; and, in many cases, the manor courts would have jurisdiction over petty offences.

These documents are an important source as more often than not they pre-date existing parish registers and can be helpful in that they list names of tenants, dates of deaths and names of heirs. They can be particularly useful in tracing successive tenants of a property and relationships between tenants. Many of the papers produced by the manorial courts provided lists of the names of suitors, jurors, tenants and petty constables, amongst others.

Although it should be remembered that the survival of Welsh manorial records varies greatly, finding those that still exist is particularly easy because all such records pertaining to Wales have been recorded on the Manorial Documents Register. The register covers court rolls, surveys, maps, customs and many other related records. If you know the name of the manor a basic search can be made; however, the advanced search facility allows you to search by county, which will then give a full list of all manors in Wales. Bear in mind that no records at all have survived for some manors and, for certain areas of Wales, the manorial system did not even exist. When you select a manor, a full list of all surviving records for that manor will be given with a description and date of the document, along with the reference number and at which repository the documents are held. The advanced search also allows you to search for particular types of records – for which a drop-down list is provided – and for a specific period. For a more in-depth account of manorial records, including a glossary and a gallery of example documents, it is well worth visiting the Cumbrian Manorial Records website – especially if you are new to using manorial records.

There are few Welsh manorial records that date to before the sixteenth century: for example, only five manorial court rolls survive from the thirteenth century. The majority of the records start in the sixteenth century and continue until the twentieth century. The manorial system was not widespread throughout Wales, but substantial records for Montgomeryshire can be found amongst the Wynnstay and Powis Castle estate papers, which are held at the National Library of Wales; those for Glamorganshire and Monmouthshire can be found in the estate papers of Badminton, Bute and Tredegar, which are also held at the National Library of Wales. Carmarthenshire was covered mostly by the twenty-five manors of the Golden Grove estate, the records of which are housed at Carmarthen Archives Service. There are also a small number of records relating to the manorial system in the north Wales counties of Anglesey, Caernarfonshire and Merionethshire.

As with all legal documents these records are written in Latin before 1733, except during the Commonwealth from 1653 to 1660, when they were written in English. Therefore, some understanding of Latin for this earlier period is required. It is recommended to look at records from the eighteenth-century or later in order to familiarize yourself with the details and layout of the records, as the earlier ones will be very similar. Very few were written in Welsh, but those that were can be found listed in an appendix to Helen Watt's book (see the further reading section).

There are three main classes of records: the court rolls or books; surveys; and the accounts. I shall only give a brief description of these, but for a more in-depth account of the records and information found within them please consult Helen Watt's book, which is the only detailed study of manorial records relating to Wales.

The court rolls are the formal records of the manor court; the earliest ones were produced on parchment rolls, but later ones were

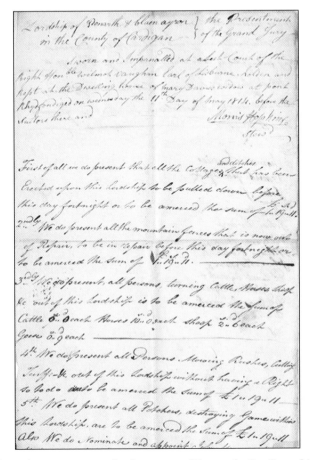

Extract from the presentments for the manor of Pennarth, Cardiganshire. (NLW, Crosswood I/1306)

written on sheets and bound in volumes. The records contain information relating to the tenants and inhabitants of a manor. Details of various courts were recorded within the rolls or books – court baron and court leet and view of frankpledge were the main ones.

Some manors were allowed to hold a court leet, which was required to meet twice a year in order to deal with certain minor offences such as breaches of the peace, poaching and assaults. It should be noted that view of frankpledge was not recorded separately in Wales as was done in England. These records were known as presentments and recorded matters such as fines for encroachments, stray animals, poaching and failure to appear in the court; the court leet was also responsible for ensuring that the manor's ditches, roads, fences, and so on, were repaired. Presentments vary from manor to manor and the following is an extract from the manor of Pennarth, Cardiganshire for May 1827 (NLW, Crosswood I/1306).

> The Court Baron administered the customs of a manor including settlement of dispute … appoint David Evans of Bronmwyn to serve the Office of Petty Constable … We present all Manner of Persons that encroach upon the Common of RhosGelly Gron are to be amerced the sum of £1.19.11 or to be pulled down immediately by the consent of the Jury …We do present all manner of Persons that dig Turffs mow rushes and Ferns on the Common. … are amerced the sum of £1.19.11 … We do present all Poachers that shoot or Trespass upon the common disturbing or killing game … to be amerced the sum of £1.19.11.

Most tenants in Wales were known as 'copyhold', which refers to the copy of the court roll entry given to the tenant. Copyholders were restricted in what they could do with their land and needed permission from the court to inherit, sell, sub-let, buy or mortgage a property. Such transactions were recorded in the court rolls and a copy was given to the tenant. The land granted by a lord would be known as tenure and the tenants would be 'free' or 'unfree'. Free tenants were required to carry out a certain type of work on the lord's land over a set period each year. An unfree tenant (or 'customary' tenant) was set a certain amount of work but the type of work would vary as necessary. The cottagers held no land but worked on the lord's land and lived in a cottage with garden. When a copyhold tenant died, a payment of a 'heriot' was made, which was also recorded. Therefore, the transfer of property through the generations can be followed via court baron records and legal disputes. The admission and surrender records within the court books record the transfer of land and property between parties and also record names and relationships of various members of a family, as in the following case found in the court book for the manor of Lanmaes, Bedford and Malefont in 1748 (NLW, Bute M5/322).

> Charles Bassett Lantwitt major yeoman youngest son and customary heir of Joan the wife of Richard Bassett who was niece and customary heir of Christopher Thomas who survived Alexander Thomas his co. Trustee and John Nicholl of Lanmaes in the said county Gentleman youngest son and customary heir of Iltid Nicholl late of the same place clerk decd two of the customary tenants of the said manor.

There are numerous examples of such records in surviving manorial collections. They can also be used alongside other manorial records such as rentals, in order to create a better and fuller picture of our ancestors' lives. Rentals very often recorded the death of a tenant and the name of a successor.

A survey would give a view of the land holdings of a particular manor at a given time. A new survey would have been undertaken if a new lord inherited or purchased the manor. This usually contains a list of tenants and occasionally includes a presentment by the jury, who would have conducted the survey in relation to the customs of the manor. A survey can also give details of inheritance; for example, it may be noted that the land was passed to the youngest son and if there was no son, to the youngest daughter – this depended on the custom of the manor.

Manorial accounts usually give details of financial matters that pertain to the running of the estate and manor, such as receipts, expenditure on farming stock and lists of wages and rentals. Survival of the records, as for all classes of manorial documents, will vary from manor to manor and between different periods.

Title deeds leave a trail of who owned a property and when; they will also refer to related documents that hold additional information. Frequently, estates grew larger through marriage between family

A rental from the Nanteos Estate, Cardiganshire, 1833. (NLW, Nanteos R64)

members from different estates; if a property suddenly appears or disappears from one estate record, the other estate should be checked. Through a continuous set of records, ancestors can be traced from one generation to the next, or the names of a property's occupants over a period of time can be ascertained. Title deeds and associated documents will provide information on the abode, the names of the residents and their occupations and relationships, and details of the extent of the property or land. The existence of many buildings within a community, such as schools, chapels and churches, were the result of agreements with or financial assistance from the gentry. These records are therefore invaluable in tracing our ancestors: where they lived, how they lived, and the growth and decline of the community around them.

This example from the Burchinshaw and Tremadog deeds is held at the National Library of Wales and relates both to the estate of the Burchinshaw family and other property in Denbighshire, and the Tremadog estate of the Roche family and other property in Caernarfonshire.

1866, April 16
ASSIGNMENT (after reciting two indentures, the first dated 17 June 1864, being a lease for 99 years at an annual rent of £22 from William Jones of Brynymor, gent., and Elias Jones of Gwiedog, farmer, to David Hughes, late of Dover House, Llandudno, and now of Penmaenmawr, painter, of a piece of land (5,445 sq. yds), part of Llwynyn Field on Brynymor Farm, bounded on the north by the new occupation road, on the east by land leased to Thomas Thomas, on the south by another portion of the said farm, and on the west by lands leased to Thomas Hughes, with a covenant for the erection by the lessee of a house and out offices at a cost of not less than £700; the other dated Oct. 1864, being an assignment from the said David Hughes to John Wynne Williams of Llandudno, grocer, of the eastern portion of the said parcel of land at an annual rent of £11, with a covenant for the erection by the assignee of a house, etc., at a cost of not less than £700, which has been performed, from the said David Hughes to Owen Griffiths of Nevill Crescent, Llandudno, builder, of the western portion of the said parcel of land for the residue of the original term of 99 years at an annual rent of £11. Consideration, £12. Witnesses: Henry Lloyd Jones, solicitor, Bangor; Morris Davies, his clerk.
Endorsed with a plan of the premises.

Estate accounts give an insight into the amount of money that was spent on wages, household expenditure, building work, maintenance and land use. Rentals give details of tenants – in many cases a succession of tenants over several generations – and should be used in conjunction with other records from the estate to build a bigger picture of the circumstances.

In 1870 a list was published of estates that were either over 3,000 acres in extent or carried an annual rental of over £3,000 per annum. The National Library of Wales holds records of fifty-four of these estates and there are records for many more within the county archive offices, along with hundreds that pertain to much smaller estates. To determine the scope and nature of an estate collection, as well as where it is held, the Archives Wales website is the best place to start.

Records from solicitors' offices may also be linked to many of the estate collections and this should be taken into account if you are researching estate records, as missing documentation or additional relevant material could be found amongst the family solicitor's documents. Many solicitors' records have been placed in the custody of the National Library of Wales or county archive offices.

Estate and manorial records can be a fascinating source for all family historians and they can be used alongside other records to create a clearer idea of how our ancestors lived; furthermore, they can also provide information when no other records are available.

Further reading
Watt, Helen, *Welsh Manors and their Records* (NLW, Aberystwyth, 2000)

Howell, David W., *Estate Records in Welsh Family History: A Guide to Research* (FFHS, 1993)

Websites
Cumbrian Manorial Records
www.lancs.ac.uk/fass/projects/manorialrecords/
Manorial Documents Register **www.mdr.nationalarchives.gov.uk**

Chapter 15

THE COURT OF GREAT SESSIONS

The records of the Court of Great Sessions have been greatly underused by family and local historians in the past, possibly due to their complexity; the daunting task of getting to grips with records; the physical size of the collection; and the lack of published information. My aim is to simplify the various classes of records that can be of use to family historians who wish to gain a greater knowledge of the collection. It is one of the most valuable of the collections held at the National Library of Wales, Aberystwyth, and is unique to Wales. For anyone interested in using Great Sessions records, Glyn Parry's book is an essential tool. It gives a detailed introduction to the Court of Great Sessions and its records before moving on to another detailed section, which provides descriptions of the documents that can be found in each of the class lists; these documents are placed in various classes, which have been given numbers or letters.

The Court of Great Sessions in Wales was established after the second Act of Union in 1542, as a result of which Wales was divided into four circuits that each included three counties. However, there was no room for Monmouthshire, therefore it was included in the Oxford circuit of English assize courts, the records of which are held at The National Archives in Kew. The four circuits that covered the counties of Wales were as follows:

- Chester: Denbighshire, Flintshire and Montgomeryshire
- North Wales: Anglesey, Caernarfonshire and Merionethshire
- Brecon: Breconshire, Glamorganshire and Radnorshire
- Carmarthen: Cardiganshire, Carmarthenshire and Pembrokeshire

The court remained in existence until its abolishment in 1830, which occurred as the result of an Act of Parliament. The formal procedure was very much like that of the assize courts in the English counties: meetings were held twice a year and each session lasted six days. The court's business was conducted in English: officials had to be English-speakers and English law was adhered to. Of the 217 judges appointed between 1542 and 1830, only thirty were natives of Wales, although some were from the border counties and may have been of Welsh descent. Prior to 1733, the official written language of the court was Latin, with a few exceptions that were written in English, such as the minutes of the court during the 1650s, witness statements in criminal actions and all equity minutes. Later records were all written in English. Deciphering the handwriting can also be difficult at times, especially as the clerks heavily abbreviated some of the records with marginal notes.

The court dealt with civil, criminal and equity cases. Every circuit court worked separately and, as a result, they each developed their own system to some extent, which explains the occasional variation in the quantity of records that have survived for each circuit. No transcripts of cases were ever made and although few of the records are of great value to genealogists, they can provide an insight into social and economic conditions at the time. The main records that may be of interest to family historians are described below.

The court spent the majority of its time hearing civil proceedings and most of the cases were disputes between individuals. The main records of civil proceedings were the plea rolls: a separate roll was made for each session. Before a plea could be included on the plea roll, an action had to reach issue: that is, both parties agreed that the matter should be heard before a jury. A plea would then include the plaintiff's complaint, known as the declaration, which was followed by the defendant's answer, known as the plea. If the matter went as far as being heard in a session, other information was also included on the plea roll such as the names of the litigants; the litigants' status and abode; details of the dispute; names of the jurors; and details of any previous trials relating to the dispute in question. However, the majority of cases related to debt. Genealogical information can sometimes be gleaned from cases relating to land disputes or in cases of deceased's estate. The plea rolls also included matters related to land, including trespass, novel disseisin and ejectment; breaches of contract; slander; and a few physical assaults. Judgements were also recorded on the plea rolls; they were usually noted immediately after a defendant's plea, or on a separate sheet, and included the damages awarded.

As there are no indexes available to the plea rolls, a date is required before the documents can be searched. If no date is known, the docket books or rolls can be used for this purpose if they have survived; they are the closest equivalent to an index for the plea rolls and include a record of all civil actions, even those that did not reach issue.

The precipe book for Cardiganshire, from 1816, lists numerous cases dealt with by the attorney Henry Lewis, which mostly relate to cases of debt. One such case is that of Isaac Jones of the parish of Llanbadarnfawr, who owed £150 to John Edwards, a smith. We can follow the case in the plea roll and the extract below documents the point where Isaac Jones denies the debt.

Isaac Jones late of the parish of Llanbadarnfawr in the said county yeoman was summoned to answer John Edwards, smith in a plea that he render unto him the sum of one hundred and fifty pounds which he owes and unjustly detains from him ... Did promise to pay the said John the said sum of one hundred and fifty pounds whenever afterwards ... Nevertheless the said Isaac although often thereunto requested the said one hundred and fifty pounds or any part thereof to the said John hath not yet paid but the same to him to pay hath hitherto refused and still doth refuse ... And the said Isaac by James Hughes his Attorney come and defends the wrong and injury when and saith that he doth not owe the said John the said sum of one hundred and fifty pounds or any penny thereof in manner and form as the said John hath above thereof complained against him ... Therefore it is commanded the sheriff of the said county that the shall cause to come before the Justices.

There are a small number of challenge pedigrees amongst the plea rolls. Their purpose was to show that the sheriff and/or coroner – who were officials empowered to summon jurors – together with their wives, were related to one or both parties that were involved in the the dispute and therefore could not act impartially. Pedigrees that showed relationships as far as the sixth degree were sometimes recited. Pedigrees entered in plea rolls are simple and unsophisticated, as they were recorded in narrative form. The appearance of such pedigrees had become scarce by the end of the seventeenth century.

If the sheriff was unable to act impartially, and as he was responsible for empanelling the jury, a pedigree would be drawn up with the aim of appointing the coroner instead of the sheriff to select a jury. The plaintiff could also challenge the coroner after successfully challenging the sheriff and, if successful again, could appoint independent electors to choose the jury. It was in the plaintiff's interest to draw challenge pedigrees in order to save time and money; according to Rice Vaughan 'he must consider and enquire whether there be any kindred, affinity or alliance between him or his wife and the Sheriff or his wife and if there be he must put his Challenge to the Sheriff' (*Practica Walliae*, p.38).

The main collection of criminal records of the Court of Great Sessions is commonly known as the 'gaol files'. Again, genealogical information is scarce, but any information gleaned can help to create a more complete picture of an individual's life. There are numerous documents amongst the gaol files, but only the most important will be mentioned here; it is worth consulting Glyn Parry's book for further information.

The gaol file usually included a calendar of prisoners, which gave an individual's name, occupation, parish and offence; occasionally a verdict was added and, when appropriate, the sentence. The calendars can be used as indexes to each session.

A bill of indictment is a document that formally charges a person with an offence. The charges were heard by one of the juries in order to decide if there was a case to be answered. These documents give the individual's name, status or occupation, their place of abode and

GLAMORGANSHIRE.

A CALENDAR

OF THE

Criminal Prisoners,

CONFINED IN HIS MAJESTY'S GAOL AT

CARDIFF;

Who are to be tried at the GREAT SESSIONS for the said County,
beginning on TUESDAY the 29th of MARCH, 1808;

BEFORE

The Honorable GEORGE HARDINGE, and ABEL MOYSEY, Esquires.

JOHN NATHANIEL MIERS, Esq. Sheriff.

Guilty
Death.-
to be Executed on Monday
april 4th

WILLIAM WILLIAMS, aged 19.—Committed 26th August, 1807, by Richard Griffiths, Esq. Coroner, charged with the wilful murder of David William, of the parish of Lantriffent.

property not proved

DAVID JONES, aged 24.—Committed 1st September, 1807, by Rowland Prichard, Esq and the Rev. Benjamin Jones, clerk, charged upon the oath of James Radcliffe, of the town of Swansea, merchant, with feloniously stealing, taking, and carrying away, one deal board of the value of six shillings and sixpence, of the goods and chattels of him the said James Radcliffe.

not proved —

WILLIAM HEATON, aged 64.—Committed 18th September, 1807, by Henry Knight, Esquire, charged upon the oath of Henry Wood, of the parish of Merthyr-mawr, with having as his clerk, and by virtue of his employment, had or received divers sums of money for and on the account of his master, the said Henry Wood; and that he the said William Heaton, did fraudulently and feloniously embezzle, and make away with the sum of one hundred and eighty pounds, thirteen shillings, and two-pence, of the monies of his said master Henry Wood, which he had so received and taken into his possession, against the form of the statute in such case made and provided.

no proof

HESTER BEYNON, aged 47.—Committed 5th November, 1807, by the Rev. Benjamin Jones, clerk, charged upon the oath of George Thomas, of the parish of Lanrhidian, on suspicion of maliciously and wilfully setting fire, on Sunday the 1st day of November, 1807, to the dwelling-house of him the said George Thomas; and also, on the further suspicion of feloniously stealing, taking, and carrying away, on the same day, from the said dwelling-house, eighty-five guineas, the property of him the said George Thomas.

no proof

JAMES BEYNON, aged, 49.—Committed 7th November, 1807, by the Rev. Benjamin Jones, clerk, charged upon the oath of George Thomas, of the parish of Lanrhidian, on suspicion of maliciously and wilfully setting fire on Sunday the 1st day of November, 1807, to the dwelling-house of him the said George Thomas; and also, on the further suspicion of feloniously stealing, taking, and carrying away, on the same day, from the said dwelling-house, eighty-five guineas, the property of him the said George Thomas.

Guilty of
Manslaughter.
12 Months Imprisonment.

JOHN JONES, otherwise JOHN, aged 22.—Committed 17th March, 1808, by James Capper, and Thomas Morgan, Esquires, Coroners for the town of Cardiff, charged with having given Henry Wheeler, of the said Town, divers mortal bruises, of which the said Henry Wheeler, at the parish of of Saint John the Baptist, in the said town, from the 20th day of January, until the 14th day of February, 1808, did languish, and languishing, did live; on which 14th day of February, the said Henry Wheeler, of the mortal bruises, aforesaid, did die.

THOMAS MORGAN, Gaoler.

J. D. BIRD, PRINTER, CARDIFF.

Calendar of prisoners held at Cardiff to be tried at the Great Sessions, 1808.
(NLW, Great Sessions 4/632/5)

details of the offence; the pleadings, verdict and sentence were often added to the document as well. However, researchers should be aware that details of the accused's place of abode, status, occupation and date of offence can be incorrect. Therefore, it is important to use the recognizances that are also kept with the gaol files, as historians believe that the information they contain is factually correct and therefore more reliable than the indictments. The documents are bonds to ensure the presence of all parties and witnesses involved at the next session, when the case would be heard in front of a jury.

For example, the following is an extract from the indictment of Maria Morris, Llanwennog, Cardiganshire, in 1795, for infanticide of her female bastard child by strangulation. No verdict was recorded in the file.

> Being big with a Female bastard child … Did bring forth the said child alive of the Body of her the said Maria Morris alone and in secret which said female child so being born alive by the laws of the Realm was a bastard … As soon as the said female bastard child was born with force and arms … Did make an assault and that the said Maria Morris with both her hands about the neck of the said child then and there fixed, her the said child then and there feloniously wilfully and of her malice afterthought did choak and strangle of which said choaking and strangling the said child then and there instantly died.

There are many witness statements within the examination papers for this particular case; one of them was John Thomas, a surgeon and man-midwife who was called to the house where Maria lived after the gardener became suspicious and suspected that she had given birth to a bastard child in the night.

The most fascinating documents amongst the files are the examinations or deposition papers. These are written accounts of interrogations and circumstantial evidence collected by the Justices of the Peace before the cases went before the court. The incidental information that can be found in these documents can provide an insight into how the people lived at the time; some of the papers record the way people dressed, as well as their working, sleeping and travelling habits.

When someone died suddenly, the death had to be investigated by a coroner, who he had to summon a jury to view the body in the place where the death had occurred. Details of coroners' inquests are included in the gaol files. The coroner was required to interview witnesses and suspects and to make sure they appeared at the next court session. The coroner was not obliged to submit his records because he was not a court official and they were deemed to be his own personal papers, but this also meant that they could be destroyed. However, their inclusion in the gaol files commences from an early date, and they are numerous: about 300 are recorded in some counties during the period between 1821 and 1830. They include inquests relating to murder, manslaughter, infanticide, suicide, unexplained deaths, accidents and disasters.

To search the gaol files, the order and minute books can be used, along with the Crown books and the black books for different circuits. The crime and punishment database on the website of the National Library of Wales is an index to the crimes, criminals and punishments that are included in the files, dating from 1730 to 1830. However, petty crimes were not usually heard before the Court of Great Sessions but by the Courts of Quarter Sessions, the records of which are usually housed in Welsh county archive offices; some additional records for Denbighshire and Montgomeryshire are held at the National Library of Wales.

The image overleaf shows the results of a search for Edward Mason, which gives his abode as Llanbadarn Fawr, Cardiganshire; his status as bargaintaker/miner (mining in this area would be lead-mining); and the details of the offence, which was the murder of Lewis Rowland by striking him with an overlay: a piece of wood used by miners.

The file number is important if you wish to view the original documents along with the document number, as this is usually the indictment number, which in this case is Great Sessions 4/903/3/16 (903 is the file number; 3 is the document number; 16 is the indictment number). Any other documents related to the case are listed at the end, in this case: Ca; I; J; Iq; R (calendar of prisoners,

Crime and punishment

New Search   1 - 1 of 1 results, arranged in chronological order.

Accused	**Edward Mason**; Parish: Llanbadarn Fawr, co. Card.; County: Cardigan; Status: Bargaintaker/miner
Offence	Murder of Lewis Rowland, Llanbadarn Fawr, miner, at Ystumtuen lead mine, by striking him with an overley. Prisoner's mother, Mary John Morris, a washerwoman of ore had ordered two miners to clear the flooring of ore. An affray ensued when deceased and two others removed ore belonging to her two sons, and threw it about. Arraigned on coroner's inquest~~ (Amendments)
Location and date	Parish: Llanbadarn Fawr, co. C; County: Cardigan; Date: 8 November 1785
Prosecutor	Unspecified
Plea	Not guilty.
Verdict	Guilty of manslaughter.
Punishment	Prays benefit of clergy fined 1/- and 1 month imprisonment.
File number	4/903/3
Document number	16
Other documents	Ca, I, J, Iq, R (Key)

Crime and punishment search result for Edward Mason (NLW)

information, jury list, inquest of coroner, recognizance); for a full list of these, you will need to click on the 'key' link.

This is an extract from the indictment of Edward Mason:

> Whereas he … Did make an assault … On him the said Lewis Rowland with a certain piece of wood called an overlay of the value of sixpence which he the said Edward Mason in both his hands then and there had a hold of the said Lewis Rowland in and upon the back part of the head … Did strike giving to the said Lewis Rowland in and upon the back part of the head of him the said Lewis Rowland with the piece of wood aforesaid one mortal bruise.

The calendar of prisoners that shows Edward Mason has annotations by the clerk which indicate that he was found guilty of manslaughter, fined one shilling and was to be imprisoned for one month.

For family historians, equity records can be useful because of the high proportion of cases that related to family disputes, including marriage settlements, wills, mortgages and land disputes. The bill books act as an index to these records, alongside the order and decree books, as they include the date of receipt of every bill of complaint. Decree and order books that have survived include details of the progress of each case and they can be used as a convenient way of discovering the outcome of a dispute. These books can provide details that include summaries of the various pleadings and other information that can be of interest to the family historian, such as valuations, property details and data concerning several generations of family members. However, it is worth noting that these records are not arranged by county but by circuit.

The pleadings are the most important records of the equity side of the court and prior to their arrival at the National Library of Wales they were separated into parchment and paper records; therefore, can be records in both groups that relate to the same case. There could be up to four stages for each equity case, which began when the bill of complaint was made by the plaintiff whilst the court was in session and was followed by the defendant's answer. This, in turn, could be returned with the plaintiff's replication and the defendant's rejoinder. However, the majority of cases ceased after the defendant's answer.

If no verdict appears in the gaol files, other means can be used to determine the outcome; the National Library of Wales holds microfilm copies of the criminal registers for Wales, covering the period from 1808 to 1892, the originals of which are held at The National Archives. These also cover the assize court cases after the abolishment of the Great Sessions in 1830. The information held on these registers is: name, when tried, crime, sentence and how it was carried out – that is, whether the defendant was discharged, acquitted, transported or imprisoned, for example. As you can see from this extract, the punishment did not always fit the crime, as we would expect in today's society. Thomas Morgan was sentenced to death for horse stealing; Thomas David was given only six months' imprisonment for manslaughter; whilst Edward Mason was merely fined a shilling, and imprisoned for one month, for manslaughter! Larceny is a crime involving the wrongful acquisition of the personal property of another person. It was an offence under the common law of England and became an offence in jurisdictions which incorporated the common law of England into their own law. It has now been abolished in England and Wales, Scotland, Northern Ireland and the Republic of Ireland. However, it still remains an offence in the United States.

Extract from the Criminal Register for the county of Cardigan, 1820, (NLW, film 854 or TNA, HO 27/1-223)

Names	When tried	Crimes	Death	Transportation	Imprisonment	Acquitals
George Powell	July session	Larceny			1 month & twice	
Morris Evans	Spring Gt Session	Having & Forged Bank Notes		14 years		
John Sprigg	Spring Gt Session	Larceny from the person				No Bill
Thomas David	Autumn Gt Session	Manslaughter			6 months	
Thomas Morgan	Autumn Gt Session	Horsestealing	Death			

There are numerous classes within the records of the Court of Great Sessions and Glyn Parry's book is strongly recommended as a source both of further detail on those that have been mentioned here and of information on those that have not.

Murray Lloyd Chapman, has transcribed the gaol files from 1541 to 1595 for the county of Montgomeryshire, and also those during the Commonwealth from 1650 to 1660. This is no mean feat and it is a fantastic source for anyone with Montgomeryshire ancestors who lived during these periods, as very few other records are available. Extensive work of this kind has not been undertaken for other counties thus far.

Further reading

Chapman, Murray Lloyd, *Criminal Proceedings in the Montgomeryshire Court of Great Sessions: Transcript of Commonwealth Gaol Files 1650–1660* (NLW & Powysland, 1996)

Chapman, Murray Lloyd, *Montgomeryshire Court of Great Sessions: Calendar of Criminal Proceedings 1541–1570* (NLW, 2003)

Chapman, Murray Lloyd, *Gaol Files 1571–1580* (NLW, 2008)

Chapman, Murray Lloyd, *Calendar of Gaol Files 1591–95* (NLW, 2010)

Chapman, Murray Lloyd, *Gaol Files 1581–90* (NLW, 2010)

Parry, Glyn, *A Guide to the Records of the Great Sessions in Wales* (NLW, 1995)

Vaughan, Rice, *Practica Walliae* (London, 1693)

Websites

National Library of Wales **www.cat.llgc.org.uk**

National Library of Wales, Crime and Punishment **www.llgc.org.uk/sesiwn_fawr/index_s.htm**

The National Archives **www.nationalarchives.org.uk**

Chapter 16

TRADE AND INDUSTRY

In this book, it would be impossible to account for even a fraction of the occupations that our ancestors worked at. However, some sources for occupational records are mentioned elsewhere, such as trade directories and apprenticeship records. Additionally, a search of the Archives Wales website will, as always, give you some idea of what is held in repositories throughout Wales – and there have been books written about many occupations, some of which are listed in the further reading section. Newspapers are also a great source of information on every aspect of social history and you will find details relating to all manner of occupations within their pages, including some that may not be documented elsewhere – and the online indexes to Welsh Newspapers Online and the British Newspaper Archive make searching easy.

We are very lucky in Wales: not only do we have the National Museum of Wales, but it is spread out over seven sites throughout the country:

- National Museum, Cardiff
- St Fagans National History Museum, Cardiff
- Big Pit National Coal Museum, Blaenavon
- National Wool Museum, Dre-fach Felindre
- National Roman Legion Museum, Caerleon
- National Slate Museum, Llanberis
- National Waterfront Museum, Swansea

One of the museum's objectives is to 'develop world-class museum spaces to inspire learning and connect people with the past, present and future'. The individual museums are highly recommended for anyone wanting to learn more about the social and industrial history of Wales.

Agriculture

Most people who research their Welsh ancestry will find connections to agriculture at some point or another. Agriculture was the main industry in Wales until the mid-nineteenth century and again later after the decline of heavy industry. Almost all records mentioned in this book will refer to those with agricultural connections, whether they were landowners, farmers, agricultural labourers or casual workers. Once you have used sources such as parish registers, nonconformist records and census returns to ascertain that your ancestors were linked to agriculture, the next step is to search for any possible connections to estate records or collections of family records in the local county archive office, or at the National Library of Wales. For example, the tithe maps and schedules will help to reveal the landowner of a particular farm in the 1840s, which, in turn, will lead to the name of the estate and the Return of Owners of Land, which was undertaken by the government in 1873. These returns showed that 60 per cent of land in Wales was owned by large estates. The nineteenth century saw pioneering changes in cultivation and the opening of the railways brought new opportunities, new markets, increased sales and therefore more profit, which was reinvested in the land.

The establishment of agricultural societies was a key element in the development of agriculture at this time. The first of these societies, the Breconshire Agricultural Society, was formed as early as 1755, and other counties followed soon after. The societies held local shows and competitions to encourage high standards. The annual agricultural shows form a key part of a farmer's local and national calendar to this day: the Royal Welsh Show, first established in 1904, is one of Europe's largest. Records for local agricultural societies – as well as friendly and benefit societies – should initially be searched for at the relevant county archive office or the National Library of Wales.

Additionally, estate records are important if your ancestors had connections with a particular estate; these records are dealt with Chapter 14.

Wool

Wales has been renowned for its wool production for hundreds of years and it was a cottage industry found in most parts of Wales. Wool was in plentiful supply throughout Wales and carding, spinning, weaving and knitting were commonplace in most areas. The wool was used to make articles of clothing and blankets; surplus items were sold to travellers, and at local markets, in order to earn money to buy other necessities. Many occupations can be associated with this industry – some of which you will come across when you search through census returns, parish registers and other sources – such as fullers, weavers, tuckers, dyers, stocking knitters, felt-hat makers, cloth merchants, tailors. The beginning of the nineteenth century saw the introduction of power-driven machines, which led to the birth of the factory-style woollen mills in Wales.

The Teifi Valley, for example, covers parts of Cardiganshire, Carmarthenshire and Pembrokeshire and was a thriving centre for the mills that produced blankets, cloth and flannel. The area was frequently referred to as the 'Huddersfield of Wales'. The National Wool Museum is situated in the old Cambrian Mills, in the heart of the Teifi Valley, at Dre-fach Felindre. The museum consists of four Grade II listed mill buildings which house historical textile-weaving machinery that can demonstrate the process of fabric production. It also has a collection of woollen textiles from mills throughout Wales, as well as a paper and photographic archive of the woollen industry. These collections are not a comprehensive record of individual mills, owners or workers, but they will give you an insight into the work of the industry. An eighteenth-century working woollen mill, Esgair Moel, has been relocated to St Fagans National History Museum, Cardiff, where there are also some archive and photographic records relating to the woollen industry in Wales.

If you are researching ancestors with connections to the woollen industry and mills in Wales, remember that local county archive offices and the National Library of Wales may hold records pertaining to the area that you are researching. For example, one of the many mills in the Teifi Valley was Bargod Woollen Mill in Dre-fach, Felindre, for which the Carmarthenshire Archive Service holds a collection of correspondence, vouchers, leaflets, advertisements, financial records and miscellaneous documents that relate to the operation and running of the mill.

As early as the seventeenth century, industrialization began in various parts of Wales with the small-scale mining of natural

Register of the North Wales Quarrymen's Union. (NLW, Ms 8743E)

elements, such as silver, lead, copper, slate, iron and coal. By the mid-nineteenth century, the Welsh had begun to understand the effects of industrialization, to the extent that by the time of the 1851 census, Wales was the first country in the world to record more people working in industry than in agriculture. Wales can therefore claim to be the world's first 'industrial nation'. Industrialists and entrepreneurs from outside the country took advantage of the rich natural resources available in Wales in order to further develop technological and engineering processes.

Slate

The slate industry in Wales can be traced as far back as Roman times, when slate was used on the roof of the fort at Caernarfon. The industry saw a continual expansion throughout the eighteenth century and rapid growth in the early nineteenth century, when slate duty was abolished and narrow-gauge railways were introduced to transport the slate to the ports, from where it was exported to England and beyond. The north-west was the hub of slate production in Wales: Penrhyn Quarry near Bethesda and the Dinorwic Quarry, near Llanberis, were two of the largest quarries in the world and Oakley Mine, near Blaenau Ffestiniog, was the largest slate mine in the world.

The decline of the slate industry began early in the twentieth century with an industrial dispute at Penrhyn Quarry, which was later followed by many of their workers enlisting to fight in the First World War. Several attractions in Wales will give you a sense of how the slate quarries and mines worked and of the lives of the workers. The National Slate Museum in Llanberis is housed in quarry buildings as well as slate-workers' cottages. The museum has a multimedia display that shows how the men and their families worked and lived. It also has the largest working waterwheel in the UK. The Llechwedd Slate Caverns at Blaenau Ffestiniog have also been converted into a major tourist attraction, where the visitor can travel deep into the mine and learn about how the slate was extracted and the lives of the miners.

In order to research aspects of the quarrying or mining of slate in north Wales, the Gwynedd Archive Service, University of Wales Bangor Archives and the National Library of Wales should be your first places to search. They hold extensive collections regarding the majority of the quarries in the area; although very few of these records, if any, will contain information relating to individuals, they are still worth checking, as you never know what you may find.

Lead

The chief lead-mining areas of Wales are in the north-east of the country: Flintshire, Denbighshire and north Cardiganshire. Lead-mining was at its height in Wales during the mid-nineteenth century.

Lead-mining usually took place in remote rural areas with very few transport links. Whole families were often engaged in the work of local lead mines, including children, and there were many other occupations that were reliant on the work that was done at these

Lead miners at Cwmystwyth lead mine, 1911. (Author's collection)

mines, such as carpenters, blacksmiths and stonemasons. Even farmworkers were enticed to work in the mines for better pay; but when work was quiet there, they would return to agricultural work. When researching records for lead mines and other industries, remember that men, women and children could be included in the documents; census returns or parish register entries may be the first evidence that you will find of these connections.

Owing to the lack of skilled labour in the field, lead-mine owners had to look further afield for the expertise they required; north Cardiganshire in particular saw the in-migration of miners from the Cornwall area due to their specialist training and their experience in the tin and lead mines. Throughout the nineteenth-century census returns of north Cardiganshire you will find an increase in surnames, such as Bray, Dunstone, Mitchel, Tregoning, Trevethan, which originated from Devon and Cornwall. Many labourers also came from Ireland, as a result of the potato famine, in the 1840s and from other mining districts in England. These migrant miners left Cardiganshire towards the end of the nineteenth century, when lead-mining entered a terminal decline because lead produced abroad had become much cheaper.

Copper

Copper-mining in Wales can be traced as far back as the Bronze Age; however, as with the mining of other natural resources in Wales, there are very few surviving records before the nineteenth century. The first copperworks was opened at Llangyfelach, Swansea, in 1717, and this began Swansea's world dominance of the copper market. Roland Puw discovered a seam of copper ore in 1768 at Parys Mountain, Anglesey, and soon it became the site of the world's most productive copper mine. By the 1850s the Swansea area was producing 75 per cent of Britain's copper and Wales was producing 50 per cent of the world's copper.

It was the smelting of copper that bought fortune to Swansea, as three times the amount of coal to ore was needed in the smelting process. Therefore, due to the abundance of coal in South Wales, copper ore was shipped from Parys Mountain and Cornwall to Swansea for smelting, before being exported globally.

Records for the Parys Mountain mine can be found amongst the collections at Bangor University, whilst the National Library of Wales holds collections of the industrial families of Nevill and Vivian in south Wales, which contain records relating to the copperworks as well as the iron and coal industries. However, there are records scattered throughout Welsh repositories. The World of Welsh Copper website describes the history of Welsh copper and includes all manner of references to the industry, such as details of the recently completed regeneration of the Hafod-Morfa Copperworks in Swansea. The improved access to the site will provide visitors with more opportunities to learn about how Swansea and the copper industry in Wales played a major part in the Industrial Revolution. Sygun and Great Orme copper mines in north Wales have also been opened as tourist attractions that tell the story of the Victorian copper miners.

Iron

Iron production did not become a major industry in Wales until the late eighteenth century: pioneering work took place in Bersham Ironworks in north-east Wales, where the use of coke rather than charcoal to smelt iron was developed. As a result, Berhsam became one of the major ironworks in Europe. In the south, Merthyr Tydfil, a small rural village at one time, became the first industrial town in Wales, due to the expansion of Cyfarthfa and Dowlais Ironworks. By south Wales was producing half of the iron exported by Britain. In fact, the south Wales coalfield was predominantly developed in response to the increase in demand for coal in the ironworks at that time. However, towards the end of the nineteenth century, steel was replacing much of the iron, especially in construction work.

Blaenavon Ironworks has now been transformed into a World Heritage Site by Cadw Welsh Historic Monuments. Many of the buildings have been restored and multimedia facilities offer an insight into the social history of Wales during a period of industrial development. Additionally, Blaenavon Community Heritage Museum has facilities for researching family history. Again, records of individual workers are probably scarce, as with the other industries, but collections of records that relate to individual ironworks can be found in county archive offices and the National Library of Wales.

Coal

As with other industries, coal has been mined in Wales for a long time, but this did not occur on a grand scale until the time of the Industrial Revolution. The market for coal was originally dominated by the demands of the iron and copper industries, as it was used in large amounts in the smelting process. By the 1830s, more coal than iron was exported from the ports of south Wales. During this period of growth, workers from Ireland, Scotland and England flocked to south Wales in search of work and this increased the population of the area considerably.

The working conditions were far from ideal and many lost their lives due to illness, accidents and underground explosions. By 1842, women, and children under the age of 10, were stopped from working underground in these mines. The Welsh Coal Mines website has a list of Welsh mining accidents, with the names of casualties in most cases. Senghenydd saw the worst mining accident in history on 14 October 1913, when 439 miners lost their lives. As with all aspects of researching the history of a coal mine or its miners, newspapers are an invaluable source of information, especially when accidents occurred or other events, such as protests and industrial action, took place.

The South Wales Miners' Library houses a comprehensive collection of resources for researching the history of the south Wales coalfield, including: books, pamphlets, journals, trade directories and yearbooks, posters, oral history recordings, and videos and banners relating to the social, cultural, educational and political histories. The Coal Owners Association was founded in 1873 and its vast collection consists of administrative records; board and committee papers; disputes records; financial records; legal records; printed and manuscript material; and statistics. These records are held at the National Library of Wales. Remember that there are very few records that relate to individual miners, but Archives Wales is a good place to start when searching for any surviving records that relate to individual coal mines.

Maritime

The majority of Wales is surrounded by the sea and it has played a very important part in shaping Welsh history. From the pirates, smugglers and explorers to the merchant ships, the Royal Navy, local fishers and lifeboat crew, people sailed from Wales to all corners of the world.

Until the arrival of the railway the sea was very often the only way to move commodities in and out of the country. It would be impossible to cover all aspects of maritime history and research, but a few useful sources will be mentioned here.

Tracing seamen can prove very difficult because usually, unless they happened to be at home at the time, they did not appear in census returns and are therefore difficult to pinpoint. The main source for merchant shipping is *Lloyd's Register of Ships*, which has been recording details of merchant vessels since 1746; the majority of the Registers can now be viewed online, or copies are available at the National Library of Wales and local archive offices. The National Archives, Kew and the National Maritime Museum, Greenwich also hold information that relates to merchant marine and naval history.

Online indexes are also available through the Crew List Index Project, which gives details of ships on particular voyages. It includes the name of the ship, details of the voyage and the cargo – and it lists the names of the crew. The Welsh Mariners Index is an online resource that lists approximately 24,000 Welsh merchant masters, mates and engineers between 1800 and 1945. Swansea Mariners also has a website that provides a global list of ships' crews, seamen, sailing ships, crew agreements and ships' logs for Swansea-registered ships.

Most archive offices in Wales hold records that pertain to maritime history. With the possible exception of Powys, the only landlocked county in Wales. Archives Wales and Welsh Newspapers Online are also great sources of information.

Records of deaths at sea either due to illness, drowning or

A view of the Bute Docks, Cardiff, 1849. (NLW, Topographical Print B8/3)

shipwrecks appear frequently in parish registers for locations along the coastline of Wales; many of the bodies are recorded as unidentified, and many others were buried far from home. Family history societies throughout Wales have recorded monumental inscriptions and these may include details of a missing ancestor lost at sea.

Further reading

Bick, David, *The Old Metal Mines of Mid Wales, Parts 1–6; 1974–1991* (Pound House, 1993)

Bick, David and Wyn Davies, Philip, *Lewis Morris and the Cardiganshire Mines* (Aberystwyth, 1994)

Brown, Jonathan, *Tracing Your Rural Ancestors* (Pen & Sword, 2011)

Carr, Tina and Schone, Annemarie, *Pigs and Ingots: The Lead/Silver Mines of Cardiganshire* (Y Lolfa, 1993)

Fitzpatrick, J. Ramsey with Kilpatrick, Felicity, *Down the Memory Lanes of My Hafod* (Brecon, 2008)

Francis, Hywel and Smith, Dai, *The Fed: A History of the South Wales Miners in the Twentieth Century* (UWP, 2004)

Hughes, Stephen, *Copperopolis: Landscapes of the Early Industrial Period in Swansea* (RCAHMW, 2005)

Jenkins, J. Geraint, *The Welsh Woollen Industry (Cardiff, 1969)*

Jenkins, J. Geraint, *Life and Traditions in Rural Wales* (2009)

Jones, R. Merfyn, *The North Wales Quarrymen, 1874–1922* (UWP, 1981)

Lewis, W. J., *Lead Mining in Wales* (UWP, 1967)

Steele, Philip and Williams, Robert, *Copper Kingdom: Parys Mountain and Amlwch's Port* (Amlwch Industrial Heritage Trust, 2010)

Tonks, David, *My Ancestor Was a Coalminer* (SOG, 2003)

Waters, Colin, *A Dictionary of Old Trades, Titles and Occupations* (Countryside Books, 2002)

Watts, Christopher T. and Watts, Michael J., *My Ancestor Was a Merchant Seaman* (SOG, 2002)

Websites

A World of Welsh Copper **www.welshcopper.org.uk**

Big Pit National Coal Museum, Blaenavon **www.museumwales.ac.uk/bigpit/**

Blaenavon World Heritage Site **www.visitblaenavon.co.uk**

Crew List Index Project **www.crewlist.org.uk**

Great Orme Copper Mine **www.greatormemines.info**

National Maritime Museum **www.nmm.ac.uk**

National Museum Wales **www.museumwales.ac.uk**

National Slate Museum, Llanberis **www.museumwales.ac.uk/slate/**

National Waterfront Museum, Swansea **www.museumwales.ac.uk/swansea/**

National Wool Museum, Dre-fach Felindre **www.museumwales.ac.uk/wool/**

Llechwedd Slate Caverns **www.llechwedd-slate-caverns.co.uk**
Lloyd's Register of Ships **www.lr.org/en/research-and-innovation**
  /historical-information/lloyds-register-of-ships-online/
South Wales Miners' Library **www.swansea.ac.uk/iss/swml/**
St Fagans National History Museum, Cardiff
www.museumwales.ac.uk/stfagan/
Swansea Mariners **www.swanseamariners.org.uk**
Sygun Copper Mine **http://www.syguncoppermine.co.uk/**
The National Archives **www.nationalarchives.gov.uk**
Welsh Coal Mines **www.welshcoalmines.co.uk**
Welsh Mariners Index **www.welshmariners.org.uk**
Welsh Mine Disasters
www.welshcoalmines.co.uk/DisastersList.htm

Chapter 17

EMIGRATION

Tradition has it that the first Welsh emigrants to the New World, Madog ab Owain Gwynedd (Prince Madog) and a group of settlers, travelled there as early as the twelfth century. However, Howell Powell, who left Brecon in 1643 for Virginia, is officially recognized as the first Welsh emigrant. During the period after the Restoration in 1660, the American colonies offered relief, along with religious and political freedom, due to the lack of religious tolerance in Wales and England. In 1663 John Miles, 'father' of the Welsh Baptists, led a group to Massachusetts. Later in 1683, Thomas Lloyd led a Quaker group from Montgomeryshire to Pennsylvania and bought 40,000 acres of land from William Penn on the outskirts of Philadelphia and further along the Delaware river. Welsh communities and societies were established throughout Pennsylvania and today it is claimed that over 200,000 inhabitants are of Welsh descent.

Some of the migration from Wales saw whole communities leaving between the seventeenth and nineteenth centuries, but it was still at a much lower rate of outward migration than that of other European countries, due to the growth of industry at home in Wales.

In their thousands, the Welsh emigrated from the ports of Liverpool, Bristol, Milford Haven and Caernarfon to New York State, and onwards to Pennsylvania and Ohio. They were attracted by the availability of land and the opportunities open to them, which were quite different to the economic hardship faced in various parts of Wales from the 1790s to the 1850s, such as failed harvests, agricultural depression and social uprisings.

The rate of Welsh emigrants peaked by the 1850s: three quarters of Welsh emigrants were from the rural areas of Carmarthenshire, Cardiganshire, Montgomeryshire and Merionethshire. The attraction was that they were promised plenty of land, higher wages, better

Poster advertising emigration to New York or Philadelphia in 1841. (NLW, Poster B1/B13) conditions, and religious and political freedom. People were encouraged to emigrate through newspaper advertisements and by friends and relatives who had already taken advantage of the promised good life.

The demand for expertise in mining – and in other industries for miners, managers and experts – led to emigration from Wales to countries across the world. Much of the emigration from Wales resulted from industrial growth in other countries. Large communities of Welsh coal miners can be found in America and Australia, but some Welsh miners also went to South Africa, China, whilst others settled closer to their homeland in Kent, England. People emigrated from Wales to other countries and continents to look for work, to improve their lives and to experience new lands and cultures, taking expertise and many traditional Welsh skills with them. The largest Welsh settlements outside of Wales were in Pennsylvania and Ohio, North America, where coal mining was very important. The copper industry in Australia, especially in Burra Burra, had Welsh connections as did the iron industry in Donetsk, Ukraine, which began as the ironworks town of Hughesovska and was funded by John Hughes of Merthyr Tydfil from 1869 to 1917. The slate quarrymen of north Wales were attracted to the Vermont area of North America and 1,500 left the Bethesda and Llanberis areas between 1845 and 1851. Other groups made their way to the sugar plantations of Barbados and Jamaica. On 13 May 1787 the First Fleet of eleven ships sailed from Plymouth to Port Jackson (Sydney), Australia, with a consignment of convicts, including four from Wales. Transportation to Australia lasted until 1868 and around 2,500 Welsh people were amongst those who endured the long voyages. Welsh missionaries also settled in Brittany, the Khasi Hills of India and Madagascar.

2015 will mark the 150th anniversary of the Welsh settling in Patagonia. In 1865, Michael D. Jones led a group of about 150 people from mid-Wales to establish a Welsh colony in Patagonia, in the Chubut Valley. They sailed on the Mimosa from Liverpool on 25 May and arrived at New Bay (Port Madryn) on 28 July. They had been led to believe that the country was very much like Wales, but they soon found that there was very little water or shelter. Nevertheless, they persevered and towards the end of the nineteenth century, the Argentine government granted the settlers title to the land. Further groups of emigrants from Wales followed and, despite many ups and downs along the way, the Welsh community still survives, with support from the Argentine and Welsh governments maintaining the Welsh heritage and language. The Welsh language and many Welsh traditions can still be experienced in the Gaiman today: including 'eisteddfodau' and 'noson lawen' (folk evening).

The Welsh built their own communities in these areas: the churches, chapels and schools were built in the traditional Welsh style; they spoke Welsh; and many street and town names reflect the presence of the Welsh in America. Although numerous Welsh societies were established throughout the world, it is also worth remembering that many Welsh people did not go as far as America, Australia or Russia, but migrated only over the border to the industrial areas of England. Welsh communities became firmly established in cities such as London and Liverpool, as well as other major towns, during the nineteenth and twentieth centuries. Many of those who emigrated did return to Wales, some for short periods of time, others for good, but some never returned and, as a result, Welsh ancestors can be found in communities all over the world. Sometimes one member of the family left to find his fortune and when established would send for his wife, children or extended family, which resulting in members of a family being scattered between Wales and other lands. This sometimes meant that branches of families lost contact with each other and a few generations down the line did not even know of the existence of family in another country. If family members seem to disappear from the records, it is worth searching to see if they went to another country.

Records of the churches, chapels and schools may well have survived and are possibly in private hands, local archives or have found their way back to Wales and are held at county archive offices or the National Library of Wales. When trying to trace ancestors in another country the same rule applies: work backwards from the known to the unknown and once a connection has been made with an area of Wales, that is the time to access Welsh records. Numerous resources have already been mentioned throughout this book, such as Welsh newspapers, many of which were published in America and Australia. Other resources include news, letters and information from those in faraway lands; commercial family history sites that hold records pertaining to British subjects who emigrated, including those who were born, married or died abroad; and passenger lists and passport information. Records in local archives and the National Library of Wales hold small personal collections of people with links to other countries, along with church, chapel and industrial records of those with Welsh connections.

One example of the material that can be found is the Ohio Project, which has digitized more than 100,000 pages of material, held at the National Library of Wales, that relates to the Welsh in Ohio, USA. It is an invaluable source for anyone that has connections with this area, as the website includes copies of *The Cambrian* magazine from 1880–1919; an index to people and places, and information about the voyage; the places where they worshipped; and the industries that were created.

Further reading
Browning, Charles H., *Welsh Tract of Pennsylvania* (Maryland, 1990)
Filby, P. William and Meyer, Mary K., *Passenger and Immigration Lists* (Detroit, Gale, 1981)
Kershaw, Roger, *Emigrants and Expats* (TNA, 2002)
Whitmore, Henry, *Genealogical Guide to the Early Settlers of America* (Baltimore, 1967)

Websites
Archives Wales **www.archiveswales.org.uk**
National Library of Wales **www.cat.llgc.org.uk**
Ohio Project **www.ohio.llgc.org.uk**
People's Collection Wales **www.peoplescollectionwales**

Chapter 18

MILITARY RECORDS

The eighteenth-century Militia Act specified the quota of able-bodied men to be provided by each county; if there were not enough volunteers, able-bodied men within each parish were balloted to take up the posts. Very often, the procedures relating to such matters will appear in the parish vestry minutes. Jeremy Gibson and Mervyn Medlycott have compiled a list that includes militia and muster rolls from Wales that have survived. These are usually held at the county archive offices, the National Library of Wales or The National Archives, but I suggest searching relevant online catalogues as well.

Service records for all army personnel before 1920 are held at The National Archives and you can find very useful information guides on the website for all aspects of military history, which also cover Wales. Bear in mind that many Welsh men and women served in regiments outside Wales and their records should also be consulted. As so much has been published on military history, some of which I have listed in the further reading section, I shall not go into great detail here other than to mention a few useful resources.

For those researching First World War, projects, websites and information will appear in abundance around the time of the centenary. Here in Wales, the Wales Remembers website, which is funded by the Welsh government and works in collaboration with many partners throughout Wales, provides news, events and information relating to the commemoration.

The National Library of Wales in partnership with Archives Wales has conducted a mass digitization of primary sources that relate to the First World War called Cymru 1914: The Welsh Experience of the First World War. The project reveals the often hidden history of all aspects of Welsh life, language and culture. The digital archive brings together material that was previously fragmented and frequently

Military images in a photo album. (Author's collection)

inaccessible, in order to create a unique resource for researchers in Wales and beyond.

Wales also has three regimental museums that document the long history of Welsh regiments, all of which are well worth a visit; the museums' websites have further information on visiting them. The Regimental Museum in Brecon was opened in 1935 and follows hundreds of years of history of the Royal Welch Fusiliers (23rd Foot). The Royal Regiment of Wales was created in 1969 by amalgamating the former 24th Foot, 41st Foot and 69th Foot and, later, the South Wales Borderers, Welch Regiment and Monmouthshire Regiment. The museum does not hold army service records for individual soldiers because these are held at the TNA (before 1920) and the

Ministry of Defence Army Personnel Centre (after 1920). A nominal fee is charged for any research undertaken by museum staff. The website has very useful FAQs, fact sheets and links to other online resources to aid you in your research. The museum's focal point is the Zulu War Room, and other displays show the involvement of the regiments in the two world wars, whilst the Medal Room houses over 3,000 medals.

The Royal Welch Fusiliers Museum has, since the 1960s, been located at Caernarfon Castle, within two of its towers. It showcases the long history of Wales' oldest infantry regiments. North Wales was the traditional home of the Royal Welch Fusiliers, but soldiers were recruited to the regiment from all over the UK and Ireland. A virtual tour of the museum can be taken from the website, which also has a useful FAQs section, fact sheets and links to other online resources, and offers a research service for a nominal fee.

On 18 Jun 2014, Cardiff Castle Museum of the Welsh Soldier opened a new exhibition entitled Firing Line; the items in the exhibition document the 300-year history of the Welsh soldiers who participated in well-known battles whilst serving in 1st The Queen's Dragoon Guards and The Royal Welsh regiments. The Royal Welsh was formed in 2006 by uniting The Royal Welch Fusiliers and The Royal Regiment of Wales (24th Foot/41st Foot). From the website you can access the military genealogy database for the 1st King's Dragoon Guards, Queen's Bay (2nd Dragoon Guards) and 1st The Queen's Dragoon Guards, which contains the names of over 19,000 soldiers. The initial surname search is free of charge and any findings will incur a £30 administration fee if you wish to access the full information. The information that can be found varies in quantity and is drawn from records held at Cardiff Castle. The service records of individual soldiers are not held on the website, but the results will be based on the occurrence of the surname within records held at Cardiff Castle. Not included on the database as yet are soldiers who served in the 41st Regiment, The 69th Regiment, The Welch Regiment and The Welsh Regiment. It is possible to research these by post and further information can also be found on the website.

Further reading

Atkinson, C. T., *The History of the South Wales Borderers 1914–18* (London, 1999; first published, 1931)

Dixon, John, *Out Since 14. A History of the 1/2nd Battalion The Monmouthshire Regiment 1914–19* (Brecon, Old Bakehouse Publications, 2000)

Dudley Ward, Major C. H. (DSO, MC), *The Welsh Regiment of Foot Guards 1915–19* (London, 1936)

Dudley Ward, Major C. H. (DSO, MC), *Regimental Records of the Royal Welch Fusiliers (formerly 23rd Foot) Vol. III 1914–18 France and Flanders* (Wrexham, 1995)

Dudley Ward, Major C. H. (DSO, MC), *Regimental Records of the Royal Welch Fusiliers (formerly 23rd Foot) Vol. IV 1915–18 Turkey, Bulgaria, Austria* (Naval & Military Press, 2006)

Fowler, Simon, *Tracing Your First World War Ancestors* (Countryside Books, 2003)

Fowler, Simon, *Tracing Your Army Ancestors* (Pen & Sword, 2013)

Gibson, Jeremy and Dell, Alan, *Tudor and Stuart Muster Rolls* (FFHS, 1989)

Gibson, Jeremy and Medlycott, Mervyn, *Militia Lists and Musters 1757–1876* (4th edn, FFHS, 2001)

Hughes, Les and Dixon, John, *'Surrender Be Damned' A History of the 1/1st Battalion the Monmouthshire Regiment 1914–18* (Caerphilly, Cwm Press, 1995)

Owen, Bryn, *History of the Welsh Militia and Volunteer Corps 1757–1908 Anglesey and Caernarfonshire* (Wrexham, Bridge Books, 1989)

Owen, Bryn, *History of the Welsh Militia and Volunteer Corps 1757–1908 Glamorgan Regiments of Militia* (Wrexham, Bridge Books, 1990)

Owen, Bryn, *History of the Welsh Militia and Volunteer Corps 1757–1908 Glamorgan Volunteers and Local Militia 1796–1816 Yeomanry Cavalry 1808–1831* (Wrexham, Bridge Books, 1994)

Owen, Bryn, *History of the Welsh Militia and Volunteer Corps 1757–1908 Vol. 3 Glamorgan, Part 2* (Wrexham, Bridge Books, 1994)

Owen, Bryn, *History of the Welsh Militia and Volunteer Corps 1757–*

1908 Carmarthenshire, Pembrokeshire and Cardiganshire, Part 1 Regiments of Militia (Wrexham, Bridge Books, 1995)

Owen, Bryn, *History of the Welsh Militia and Volunteer Corps 1757–1908 Denbighshire and Flintshire, Part 1 Regiments of Militia* (Wrexham, Bridge Books, 1997)

Owen, Bryn, *Images of Wales: The Welch Regiment (41st and 69th Foot) 1881–1969* (Cardiff, The Welch Regiment Museum, 1999)

Owen, Bryn, *History of the Welsh Militia and Volunteer Corps 1757–1908 Montgomeryshire Regiments of Militia Volunteers and Yeomanry Cavalry* (Wrexham, Bridge Books, 2000)

Retallack, John, *The Welsh Guards* (London, Frederick Warne, 1981)

Thomas, Garth, *Records of the Militia from 1757* (PRO Guide No. 3 1993)

Wyn Griffith, Llewelyn, (ed. Riley, Jonathan) *Up to Mametz and Beyond* (Pen & Sword, 2010)

Websites

Cardiff Castle: Museum of the Welsh Soldier
www.cardiffcastlemuseum.org.uk
Imperial War Museum **www.iwm.org.uk**
The Regimental Museum of The Royal Welsh (Brecon)
www.royalwelsh.org.uk
The Royal Welch Fusiliers Museum, located at Caernarfon Castle
www.rwfmuseum.org.uk

Chapter 19

LAND TAX ASSESSMENT RECORDS

Land tax assessment records can be of use to family historians for the period before the introduction of civil registration, census returns and when parish registers are missing. They can give an indication of the succession of occupiers of a property, and changes in occupiers' names can indicate a death or a change of residence. The assessments should be used alongside other sources, as it is generally believed that they are not always accurate and that many small landowners did not appear in the lists.

Land tax was first collected in England and Wales in 1693 and was not abolished until 1963. It was collected on a local basis and collection areas were arranged by county, hundred, parish, and township when necessary. Relatively few records pre-date 1780 in Wales and most surviving records are from the years between 1780 and 1832. It was during this period that copies of the land tax assessments were placed within the Quarter Sessions records in order that clerks of the peace could use them to determine a person's electoral rights before Parliament introduced the Reform Act in 1832. Therefore, records can be found at the county archive offices or, in the case of Cardiganshire, there is an extensive collection in the Roberts and Evans papers held at the National Library of Wales.

From 1772 onwards, the lists should include all owners and occupiers of land, but this was not always the case, as it was not until 1780 that the lists were kept more regularly. Early assessments hold very little information: usually only the proprietor's or occupier's name (it is not always clear which) and the amount of tax paid quarterly or annually. Property details were not usually given; however, there are exceptions amongst the few that have survived from before 1780 and these are always worth checking, as shown in the extract below, 'the town and liberties of Carnarvon 1720'

Land tax assessment for Caron Uwch Clawdd parish, Cardiganshire, 1795. (NLW, Roberts and Evans, 56/9/2)

(Nanhoron 184–86). Bear in mind that when using these lists, other sources would need to be checked in order to find out if these are the names of the proprietors or occupiers.

	£	s	d
Richard Williams for Sckibor-wen	01	01	03
Hugh Jones Curier for Cae bach	00	01	00
John Thomas Owen for Maes y barker			
& green groft	00	10	07
John Griffith Esqr for Pen y Gelly	00	10	07
Ditto for Bedows Lands	00	04	03
Ditto for Cae Lonegay	00	02	01

From 1798, printed forms were created but many parishes still used handwritten forms until a much later date. The forms included the number of the register; the names of proprietors; the names of the occupiers; the sums assessed; and the date of the contract. It is generally thought that details of the property were not included in the 1798 assessments; however, it has been found that many areas of Wales did indeed include property details and that some also included occupation on the list. The following is an extract from the 1798 assessments for the parish of Llanavan and Westra in Cardiganshire (TNA, Class IR 23/113):

No. of Register	Names of Proprietor	Names of Occupiers And Tenements	Sums Assessed			Contract Date
			£	s	d	
	Earl Lisburne	Crosswood Morris Hopkins	2	15	3	
	Earl Lisburne	Trawscoed ucha Morris Hopkins		11	4	
	Earl Lisburne	Tynyfron Sir Thos Bonsall		8	1	
	Earl Lisburne	Pantyrhaidd Sir Thos Bonsall		4	10	
	Earl Lisburne	Lodge and Fields John Evans	1	7	7	

A uniform record for the whole of England and Wales, except for Flintshire, for the year 1798 is held at The National Archives, Kew, in Class IR 23. The class comprises 121 volumes in total. The National Library of Wales holds microfilm copies of the volumes pertaining to Wales, including Monmouthshire (NLW, films 900–903). Local county archive offices may also hold microfilm copies of the volumes that relate to their own counties.

From 1798, landowners could choose to be redeemed or exonerated from payment of the land tax if they agreed to pay a lump sum payment that was equivalent to fifteen years of tax. This could be paid in one sum or in instalments. Those exonerated were noted as such on the returns from 1798 until 1832, after which they did not appear in the lists. Dates for the exoneration contracts appear in Class IR 23, and the Parish Books of Redemptions (Class IR 22) give further details of exonerated land along with the full contracts that appear in Class IR 24.

From 1832, many assessments continued to be lodged with the clerks of the peace, even though they were no longer used for voting purposes. Therefore, the number of surviving records dating from 1832 onwards is again variable. For a full list of the surviving records and in which repository they are held, see the work by Jeremy Gibson, Mervyn Medlycott and Dennis Mills. The guide will also give you much more information on the contents of the assessments and how to interpret them.

Further reading
Gibson, Jeremy, Medlycott, Mervyn and Mills, Dennis, *Land and Window Tax Assessments* (FFHS, 1998)

Websites
National Library of Wales **www.llgc.org.uk**
The National Archives **www.nationalarchives.org.uk**

Chapter 20

OTHER SOURCES

Bidding Letters

The bidding letter shared many characteristics with the 'stori wadd' (bidding story), whereby a 'gwahoddwr' or bidder was appointed by the bride's family to call at the houses of friends and acquaintances to orally deliver the invitation to the wedding ceremony and feast. But the letter lacked the 'hwyl' (fun) and humour of the oral tradition. The bidding letter increased in popularity from the end of the eighteenth century and continued throughout the nineteenth century, but the practice of both traditions had declined dramatically by the beginning of the twentieth century.

South-west Wales was the area where the tradition was predominantly found: that is, the whole of Carmarthenshire with bordering areas of Cardiganshire, Pembrokeshire, Glamorganshire and Breconshire. The bidding letter was produced by local printers and was an invitation to the wedding, which would usually have been held at the home of the bride's parents. It would request gifts for the bride and groom and reciprocation of gifts previously given by the bride and groom's parents and family members to other betrothed couples. As a result, the names and relationships of many family members would be included in the letter; therefore, this information is of interest to family historians as it can open other avenues of research if details of parents, grandparents, step-parents, siblings or other relatives were included. The bride and groom were partly dependent on these gifts and money in order to set up home.

The bidding could take place at any time; it usually occurred on the wedding day, but could take place after that date. A record would

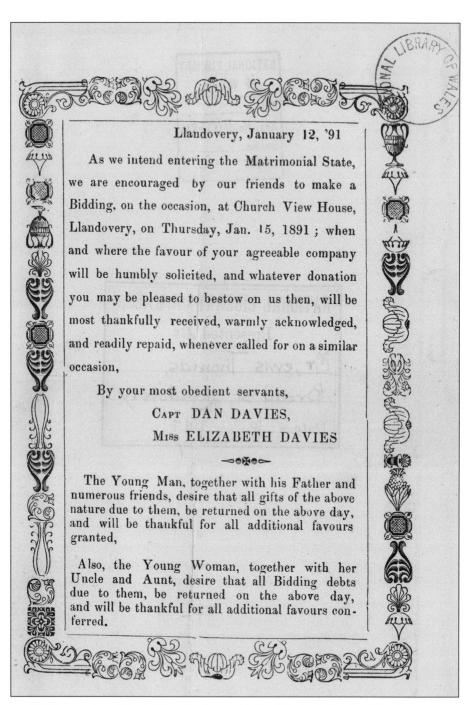

Bidding poster of Capt. Dan Davies and Miss Elizabeth Davies, Llandovery, Carmarthenshire, 1891. (NLW, Poster A3/41)

be kept of the names and donations given by all in a special bidding account book. Around 500 bidding letters are known to have survived throughout Wales but, unfortunately, only a dozen or so account books are still in existence. Collections of bidding letters and account books are held at the National Library of Wales and the Carmarthenshire Archives; however, other local archive offices may have a small number in their collections, so it is always worth asking. Digital images of a few samples can be found on the People's Collection Wales website.

Here is a transcript of a bidding letter, which can be viewed at the People's Collection Wales website or at the Carmarthenshire Archives Service. The letter illustrates the information that can be found in such a source:

Carmarthenshire July 8th, 1872

As we intend to enter the MATRIMONIAL STATE on FRIDAY, the 9th day of AUGUST next, we are encouraged by our Friends to make a BIDDING on the occasion, at the Young Woman's Father's house, called BLAEN-NANT-Y-MAB, in the Parish of Llanegwad, when and where the favour of your good and agreeable company is most respectfully solicited.

By your most obedient servants

DAVID THOMAS
ROSA DICKINS

—————————O—————————-

The young Man, together with his Father and Mother, William and Mary Thomas, Pantyrewig, his sister, Jane, his brother and sister-in-law, Evan and Margaretta Thomas, Cilarddu, his brother-in-law and sister, David and Sarah Griffiths, Ty'nyffordd, desire that all Bidding debts due to them, be returned to the young man n the above day, and will be thankful for all additional favours granted.

The young Woman, together with her Father and Mother, Edward and Rachel Dickins, Blaennantymab, her sister, Jane, her Uncle and Aunt, Morgan and Elizabeth Price, Llanfynydd desire that all Bidding debts be returned to the Young Woman the above day, and will be thankful, together with her cousins John Evans, Ferry Farm and Evan and Esther Evans, Cefn, Llanegwad for all additional favours granted.

The Young Woman's Father will repay all Bidding Debts bestowed on the Young couple on the above day whenever called upon to do so on a similar session.

THE YOUNG MAN'S FRIENDS WILL MEET AT PANTYREWIG

Trade Directories

Trade and commercial directories are one of the great sources of information for Wales, and directories were published as early as the beginning of the nineteenth century. Pigot's, which was one of the most popular, started publishing in 1814; others that were common in Wales were Slater's, Kelly's and the Post Office directories. These are usually divided into north Wales, south Wales and mid-Wales editions. The earlier ones, which were created for the main towns and cities only, did not contain much information other than listing tradesmen and other professionals and giving their addresses; however, by the 1830s the more rural parts of Wales were also included when the directory companies engaged the services of agents and local informants to gather information. They are always slightly out of date due to the time that lapsed between the information being gathered and the directory being published, but they are a great source for tracing addresses and residents in between census returns.

The later directories give detailed descriptions both of urban and rural areas and they give geographical descriptions, historical information and statistics; they also include the names and addresses of private residents, officials, craftsmen, farmers, carriers and others, along with details of local postal services, schools, workhouses and railways. The main listings give the names of public houses and posting inns, as well as a list of carriers that states their names and the times of their arrivals and departures. Not all householders were included: only prominent members of the community, local traders and professionals. The directory also included many trade advertisements, so you can check these to see if your ancestor is featured.

It is worth searching several years' worth of directories, and also those by different publishers, as details may vary from one publication to another depending on the source of the information. Some individuals could appear several times and they might appear under residents' listings as well as those for trades or professions; others may have more than one profession and may appear under the different trade titles. Of course, people often changed occupations, so whenever possible a series of directories should be consulted, alongside census returns and other sources, in order to obtain a fuller picture of the working life of your ancestor.

A selection of directories can be found in most public libraries and local record offices, which will mostly cover their own areas. The National Library of Wales holds a comprehensive collection of directories; therefore, consulting their online catalogue for holdings is recommended. The University of Leicester provides a searchable database for nineteenth-century directories at www.historical directories.org, which includes fifty-four directories that cover all dates and all parts of Wales. Although it is not a complete collection of directories for Wales, it is a very good starting point and gives free access to digital images of the pages. A selection of twelve directories that cover various parts of Wales can also be found on Ancestry.

An extract from *Kelly's Directory of Monmouthshire and South Wales*, 1895:

LLANFIHANGEL YSTRAD is a parish in the county of Cardigan, on the river Aeron, $7^1/_2$ miles from Lampeter, the nearest station, on the Manchester and Milford railway, $5^1/_2$ south-east from Aberayron, and 22 from Aberystwith, in the hundred of Moyddyn, petty sessional division of Ilar Lower and Aberayron, county court district and union of Aberayron, and in the rural deanery of Glyn Aeron, archdeaconry of Cardigan and diocese of St David's. The church of St Michael is a plain building of stone, consisting of chancel, nave and north aisle and a turret with spire, containing 1 bell. The church was restored in 1878 at a cost of £1,500 and affords 200 sittings. The registers date from the year 1685. The living is a vicarage, tithe rent-charge £132; average £98, with glebe (£23), net income £142, in the gift of the bishop of St David's, held since 1867 by the Rev. Evan Morgan of St David's College, Lampeter. At Cribin, 4 miles distant, is a chapel of ease, erected in 1894. There is also a Congregational Chapel and two Unitarian Chapels. Captain Vaughan is the principal landowner. The soil is light and slately; chief crops, wheats and oats. The area is 7,649 acres; rateable value £4118, the population in 1891 was 976.

Letters are received through Talsarn RSO, Cardiganshire at 9.15am and dispatched same time. The nearest post, money order & telegraph office is at Talsarn.
A School Board of 7 members was formed 31 March 1874, E Evans, Rhydybont, Ciliau Aeron, clerk; David Price Jones, attendance officer.
Board School (mixed) built for 180 children; average attendance 171; Thomas Davies, master.

PRIVATE RESIDENTS
Lewes, Col. Jn. D. L., J.P., Llanlear
Morgan, Rev. Evan, vicarage
Rawlins, Major-Gen. Alexander, Brynog

COMMERCIAL
Davies, David, farmer, Lloydgack
Evans, Thomas, farmer, Greengrove
Howells, David, grocer
Jenkins, Jenkin, farmer, Llanwern

Lloyd, Thomas, blacksmith
Rees, John, Vale of Aeron, P.H. [Public House]
Richards, Daniel, Brnog Arms, P.H.

Poll books and Electoral Lists

Poll books date from the end of the seventeenth century and list the names of those that were entitled to vote in the parliamentary county and borough elections. They list the names of voters and their places of residence; they also showed how they voted, as this was done publicly until the introduction of the secret ballot, through the Ballot Act of 1872. Few men had the right to vote because, in order to qualify, they had to be over the age of 21 and were required to have freehold land or tenements with the annual value of 40 shillings or more. The poll books listed the place of residence and often included the address of the qualifying property and the occupation of the voter, which can be useful for family historians.

The list of voters was arranged by parish, ward, hundred or township and, until 1832, Welsh counties returned one MP – except for Monmouthshire, which returned two. Welsh boroughs often shared an MP with a neighbouring borough. Since 1711, the poll books have been in the hands of the clerks of the peace and, as a result, many more have survived after this date. The last true poll book that showed how men voted dates from 1868 because the secret ballot was introduced in 1872, after which the information was no longer published.

Surviving poll books for Wales can be found at the National Library of Wales; the Department of Manuscripts, University College of North Wales, Bangor; and local county archive offices. For a detailed list of which records are available and where they are held, consult the work of Jeremy Gibson and Colin Rogers.

The following is an example of information that can be found and is an extract from the Monmouth Poll Book of 1835 (NLW, Twiston Davies 4724); the candidates were Benj. Hall, Esq. and Joseph Bailey, Jun., Esq. The 'H' column is for Hall votes and the 'B' column for Bailey votes.

			H	B
Embry, Thomas	Gent.	Grinder-Street	–	
Evans, Robert	Gent.	Monnow-Street		–
Evans, George	Farmer	Penalt		–
Edwards, Charles	Mason	Market-place		–
Edwards, John	Malster	Grinder-street		–
Evans, Charles	Baker	Church-street	–	

Electoral registers were first published in 1832 after the introduction of the Reform Act, which made it compulsory for local authorities to produce annual registers of voters. They have been published annually since, except for the years 1916–1917 and 1940–1944.

These differ slightly from the poll books, as people were unable to vote unless their names were included in the register; furthermore, entitlement to be included on the register was based on the amount of land owned, although the requirements varied over the years. In borough elections, male householders, including tenants of land worth £10 a year, were allowed to vote, but only owners of property were entitled to vote in county elections. This qualifying amount of land value was lowered to £5 in 1867. By 1884, the majority of male householders over 21 were entitled to vote. However, it was 1918 before women were given the vote and even then it was limited to those aged 30 or over, although this was lowered to the age of 21 in 1928.

The 1832 Reform Act extended qualification in county elections even further:

> • to anyone who had a life interest in and occupation of lands or tenements worth over £2 and under £5 per annum;
> • to all other holders of real property worth at least £10; this was reduced to £5 by the 1867 Reform Act, which also gave the vote to men who were occupiers (owners or tenants) of lands that had a rateable value of £12 or more, and were paying poor rates;
> • to occupiers, as tenants of lands or tenements, who paid rent of £50 per annum or more.

The electoral registers listed the name and address and qualification to vote, sometimes lists of owners and occupiers were shown in different lists, but they were all arranged alphabetically by surname. All registers are dated 1 January, but the qualifying date to be included was usually 31 July; therefore, when searching for family members, bear this in mind, as electors could have moved or died between these dates. Electoral registers can be useful for tracing families after the 1911 census; if an address has been established, it will be possible to search for the residence in the annual electoral registers in order to see how long family members were resident in a property.

Electoral registers for Wales can be found in numerous collections, amongst them the National Library of Wales; The National Archives; The British Library; and of course county archive offices. For a detailed account of surviving registers up to 1948, consult the work of Jeremy Gibson, which includes an exhaustive re-examination of electoral registers held at the National Library of Wales.

Here are some extracts from typical electoral registers, which show the various qualifications to vote:

Voters in respect of Property – including Tenant Occupiers at a Rent of £50 and upwards

Electoral Register of the parish and polling district of Llandisilio, Montgomeryshire 1874. (NLW, Longueville 1355)

Christian name and surname of each voter at full length	Place of abode	Nature of qualification	Street, Lane or other like place in this parish
Davies, Charles Llewelyn	Trewyllan, Llansanffraid	Freehold Land	Rhysnant Township
Davies, David	Cefn Briw	Freehold house and land	Sychpwll, Haughton
Davies, Thomas	Church House	Land as occupier	Sychpwll, Haughton
Dickin, George Lloyd	Tyndwfr, Llangollen	Freehold annuity or rent charge	Tenement and land called the Canal House, John Dickin Esq. Proprietor
Downes, Richard	Carnbwll	Farm and land as occupier	Carnbwll

*Examples from the township of Parcel Canol, Aberystwyth
Polling District, Cardiganshire, 1863.
(NLW, Minor Deposit 577B)*

Christian name and surname of each voter at full length	Place of abode	Nature of qualification	Street, Lane or other like place in this parish
Edwards, John	Blaengeuffordd	Lease for 60 years	Blaengeuffordd
Griffiths, John	Llanbadarn	Freehold property	Dolcniw
Griffiths, William	Melinhen	Lease for lives of of a farm	Melinhen
Jones, John	Rhosgoch	Occupier as tenant of a farm above £50 rent	Rhosgoch
James, Richard	Broncastell	Freehold farms	Lluestfawr, J Edwards, tenant
Morgan, John	Dolberllan	Leasehold cottages	Dolberllan
Rowland, David	Trefeglwys	Mortgagee in possession of land	Nantymoch, James James, tenant
Thomas, John	Blaengeuffordd	Lease of cottage for 60 years	Blaengeuffordd

Eisteddfod

The National Eisteddfod of Wales is the country's premier cultural festival. It is held during the first week of August each year and its location alternates between the north and south of Wales. It is a festival of song, dance, poetry and art in the Welsh language. Highlights of the week are the two main ceremonies of chairing and crowning of the bard held by the Gorsedd of the Bards. The Urdd (Welsh Youth Movement) also holds annual local and regional festivals, as well as a national eisteddfod, which also travels to various parts of Wales.

The first record of an eisteddfod dates back to 1176, when a festival was held by Lord Rhys at Cardigan. Very little mention is made of it again until the sixteenth century, the time of the 'Beirdd yr Uchelwyr' (Poets of the Gentry), when the bards and musicians competed to be the best in their field. The decline of the poets of the gentry also saw a decline in the eisteddfod until it was reignited again in the nineteenth century and continues to thrive today. The literary competitions of poems and prose were submitted under a 'ffugenw' (pseudnonym) and members of the Gorsedd were, and still are, known by bardic names. Poets also published their work in newspapers under these names.

You may find that one of your ancestors was a poet or literary writer, or you may have come across pseudonyms within your research that seemed to be of little significance. Over the past two centuries, the National Eisteddfod has been joined by much smaller local 'eisteddfodau' and 'cyrddau cystadleuol' (competitive meetings). You may discover works amongst family documents, in local archives, or at the National Library of Wales, where the papers of The National Eisteddfod of Wales are held. If an ancestor was known to have competed or won at one of the National Eisteddfodau, the piece may be amongst those held at the National Library of Wales. Otherwise, local newspapers may contain results of local eisteddfodau and publication of poetical works. Many of the small bards privately published their works locally and the catalogue of the National Library of Wales or the holdings of the local library should be considered. Many of the Welsh language newspapers regularly had poetry columns that featured submissions from readers using a pseudonym. Compositions for local eisteddfodau or newspaper columns are usually in Welsh and may well include topics such as a person, a place, the commemoration of a birth, marriage, death or other occasion.

The Eisteddfod Chair is given for the best 'awdl' on a given topic. An 'awdl' is poetry written in a strict metre form known as 'cynghanedd'. The Crown is given for the best 'pryddest': poetry written in free verse on a given topic. One of the best known poets of recent times was 'Hedd Wyn' (his bardic name) alias Ellis Humphreys Evans. He was was killed during the Battle of Passchendaele in the First World War and was posthumously awarded the Chair in the 1917 National Eisteddfod. The work for

Announcing the 1952 National Eisteddfod in Aberystwyth. (NLW, Geoff Charles Collection)

which he received this award was an 'awdl' entitled 'Yr Arwr' (The Hero), written under his pseudonym, 'Fleur de Lys'. His chair was draped in a black cloth and the 1917 Eisteddfod is often referred to as the 'Eisteddfod y Gadair Ddu' (The Eisteddfod of the Black Chair).

Further reading

Gibson, Jeremy, *Electoral Registers 1832–1948; and Burgess Rolls* (FHP, 2008)

Gibson, Jeremy and Rogers, Colin, *Poll Books 1696–1872: A Directory to Holdings in Great Britain* (4th edn, FHP, 2008)

Websites

Archives Wales **www.archivewales.org.uk**

Carmarthenshire Archive Service
www.carmarthenshire.gov.uk/english/leisure/archives/pages/archivesrecords.aspx

National Library of Wales **www.cat.llgc.org.uk**

National Museum Wales **www.museumwales.ac.uk**

People's Collection Wales **www.peoplescollectionwales**

The National Eisteddfod of Wales **www.eisteddfod.org.uk**

Welsh Newspapers **welshnewspapers.llgc.org.uk**

Appendix 1

LDS Family History Centres in Wales

It is recommended that you telephone in advance of visiting to make an appointment, as opening times vary. Check online for up-to-date information at http://www.londonfhc.org/content/other-uk-centres

CARDIFF
Heol-y-Deri, Heol Llanishen Fach, Rhiwbina, Cardiff, South Glamorgan, CF14 6UH;
tel: 02920 625342

CHESTER
Aled House, Lakeside Business Village, St David's Park, Ewloe, Flintshire, CH5 3XA;
tel: 01244 548710

CWMBRAN
The Highway, Croesceiliog, Cwmbran, NP44 2NH;
tel: 01633 483856

GAERWEN
Holyhead Road, Gaerwen, Anglesey, LL60 6DB;
tel: 01248 421894 or 01248 440809

MERTHYR TYDFIL
Nant y Gwenith Street, George Town, Merthyr Tydfil, CF48 1BS;
tel: 01685 722455

NEWCASTLE EMLYN
Cardigan Road, Newcastle Emlyn, Carmarthenshire, SA38 9RD;
tel: 01239 711472

RHYL
171 Vale Road, Rhyl, Denbighshire, LL18 2PH;
tel: 01745 331172 or 01745 561209

SWANSEA
Cockett Road, Swansea, SA2 0FH;
tel: 01792 585 792

Appendix 2

Translation Tables

Numbers

1	un	11	un ar ddeg/un deg un
2	dau (dwy)	12	deuddeg/un deg dau
3	tri (tair)	13	tri ar ddeg/un deg tri (tair)
4	pedwar (pedair)	14	pedwar ar ddeg/un deg pedwar
5	pump	15	pymtheg/un deg pump
6	chwech/chwe	16	un ar bymtheg/ un deg chwech
7	saith	17	dau (dwy) ar bymtheg/ un deg saith
8	wyth	18	deunaw/un deg wyth
9	naw	19	pedwar (pedair) ar bymtheg/un deg naw
10	deg	20	ugain/dau ddeg

Days of the week

Dydd Llun	Llun	Monday
Dydd Mawrth	Maw.	Tuesday
Dydd Mercher	Mer.	Wednesday
Dydd Iau	Iau	Thursday
Dydd Gwener	Gwen.	Friday
Dydd Sadwrn	Sad.	Saturday
Dydd Sul	Sul	Sunday

Months of the year

Ionawr	Ion.	January
Chwefror	Chwe.	February
Mawrth	Maw.	March
Ebrill	Ebr.	April
Mai	Mai	May
Mehefin	Meh.	June
Gorffennaf (Gorphennaf)	Gorff. (Gorph.)	July
Awst	Awst	August
Medi	Medi	September
Hydref	Hyd.	October
Tachwedd	Tach.	November
Rhagfyr	Rhag.	December

Counties

Sir Aberteifi	Aberteifi	Cardiganshire
Sir Benfro	Penfro	Pembrokeshire
Sir Ddinbych	Dinbych	Denbighshire
Sir Drefaldwyn	Trefaldwyn	Montgomeryshire
Sir Faesyfed	Maesyfed	Radnorshire
Sir Feirionnydd	Meirionnydd	Merionethshire
Sir Fôn	Môn	Anglesey
Sir Forgannwg	Morgannwg	Glamorganshire
Sir Frycheiniog	Brycheiniog	Breconshire
Sir Fynwy	Mynwy	Monmouthshire
Sir Gaerfyrddin	Caerfyrddin	Carmarthenshire
Sir Gaernarfon	Caernarfon	Caernarfonshire
Sir y Fflint	Fflint	Flintshire

Appendix 3

Register Offices in Wales

ARDUDWY
The Register Office, Bryn Marian, Church Street, Blaenau
Ffestiniog, Ardudwy, LL41 3HD; tel: 01766 830217

BANGOR
The Register Office, Town Hall, Bangor, LL57 2RE;
tel: 01248 362418

BLAENAU GWENT
The Register Office, The Grove, Church Street, Tredegar, NP22
3DS; tel: 01495 722305; email: registrars@blaenau-gwent.gov.uk

BRECONSHIRE
Neuadd Brycheiniog, Cambrian Way, Brecon, Powys, LD3 7HR;
tel: 01874 624334

BRIDGEND
The Register Office, Sunnyside, Bridgend, CF31 4AR;
tel: 01656 642391; email: registrar@bridgend.gov.uk

CAERNARFON
The Register Office, Swyddfa Arfon, Penrallt, Caernarfon,
LL55 1BN; tel: 01286 682661

CAERPHILLY
The Register Office, Ystrad Fawr, Ystrad Mynach, Hengoed,
CF82 7SF; tel: 01443 863478; email: registrars@caerphilly.gov.uk

CARDIFF
The Register Office, 48 Park Place, Cardiff, CF10 3LU;
tel: 029 2087 1690; email: registrars@cardiff.gov.uk

CARDIGANSHIRE CENTRAL
The Register Office, 21 High Street, Lampeter, SA48 7BG;
tel: 01570 422558

CARDIGANSHIRE NORTH
The Register Office, Canolfan Rheidol, Rhodfa Padarn, Llanbadarn
Fawr, Aberystwyth, SY23 1UE; tel: 01970 633580/582

CARDIGANSHIRE SOUTH
The Register Office, Glyncoed Chambers, Priory Street, Cardigan,
SA43 1BZ; tel: 01239 612684

CARMARTHEN
The Register Office, Parc Myrddin, Richmond Terrace, Carmarthen,
SA31 1DS; tel: 01267 228210;
email: registrars@carmarthenshire.gov.uk

CONWY
The Register Office, The Town Hall, Lloyd Street, Llandudno,
Conwy, LL30 2UP; tel: 01492 576624;
online indexes: NorthWalesBMD

DE MEIRIONYDD
The Register Office, Council Offices, Cae Penarlag, Dolgellau,
LL40 2YB; tel: 01341 422341; online indexes: NorthWalesBMD

DENBIGHSHIRE NORTH
The Register Office, Morfa Clwyd, Marsh Road, Rhyl,
Denbighshire, LL18 1AF; tel: 01745 366610;
online indexes: NorthWalesBMD

DENBIGHSHIRE SOUTH
The Register Office, Town Hall, Wynnstay Road, Ruthin, Denbighshire, LL15 1YN; tel: 01824 706187; online indexes: NorthWalesBMD

DWYFOR
The Register Office, Cob Road, Pwllheli, LL53 5AA; tel: 01758 704078

FLINTSHIRE
The Register Office, Llwynegrin Hall, Mold, Flintshire, CH7 6NR; tel: 01352 703333; email: registrars@flintshire.gov.uk; online indexes: NorthWalesBMD

HAY
The Borough Council Offices, Broad Street, Hay-on-Wye, Powys, HR3 5BX; tel: 01497 821371

LLANELLI
The Register Office, 2 Coleshill Terrace, Llanelli, SA15 3DB; tel: 01554 744202; email: registrars@carmarthenshire.gov.uk

MACHYNLLETH
The Register Office, 11 Penrallt Street, Machynlleth, Powys, SY20 8AG; tel: 01654 702335

MERTHYR TYDFIL
The Register Office, Ground Floor, Castle House, Glebeland Street, Merthyr Tydfil, CF47 8AT; tel: 01685 723318; email: registrars@merthyr.gov.uk

MID POWYS
The Register Office, Powys County Hall, The Gwalia, Ithon Road, Llandrindod Wells, LD1 5LG; tel: 01597 826020; email: registrar@powys.gov.uk; online indexes: NorthWalesBMD

MONMOUTH
The Register Office, Coed Glas, Coed Glas Lane, Abergavenny,
NP7 5LE; tel: 01873 735435;
email: registeroffice@monmouthshire.gov.uk

NEATH PORT TALBOT
The Register Office, 119 London Road, Neath, SA11 1HL;
tel: 01639 760021

NEWPORT
The Register Office, 8 Gold Tops, Newport, South Wales,
NP20 4PH; tel: 01633 414770; email: registrar@newport.gov.uk

NEWTOWN
The Register Office, Council Offices, The Park, Newtown, Powys,
SY16 2NZ; tel: 01686 627862

PEMBROKESHIRE
The Register Office, Tower Hill, Haverfordwest, SA61 1SS;
tel. 01437 775176; email: registrars@pembrokeshire.gov.uk

PENLLYN
The Register Office, Fron Fair, High Street, Bala, LL23 7AD;
tel: 01678 521220; online indexes: NorthWalesBMD

RADNORSHIRE EAST
The Register Office, 3 Station Road, Knighton, Powys, LD7 1DU;
tel: 01547 520758

RHONDDA CYNON TAF
The Register Office, Courthouse Street, Pontypridd, CF37 1LJ;
tel: 01443 486869; email: registrar@rhondda-cynon-taff.gov.uk

SWANSEA
The Swansea Register Office, County Hall, Oystermouth Road,
Swansea, SA1 3SN; tel: 01792 636188;
email: registrars@swansea.gov.uk

TORFAEN
The Register Office, Hanbury Road, Pontypool, Torfaen NP4 6YG;
tel: 01495 762937; email: registrars@torfaen.gov.uk

VALE OF GLAMORGAN
The Register Office, Holton Road, Barry, CF63 4RU;
tel: 01446 709490;
email: registrationservice@valeofglamorgan.gov.uk

WELSHPOOL AND LLANFYLLIN
Neuadd Maldwyn, Severn Road, Welshpool, Powys, SY21 7AS;
tel: 01938 552228

WREXHAM
The Register Office, Ty Dewi Sant, Rhosddu Road, Wrexham, LL11
1NF; tel: 01978 292027; online indexes: Wrexham County Borough
Council, NorthWalesBMD and CheshireBMD

YNYS MÔN
The Register Office, Shire Hall, Glanhwfa Road, Llangefni,
Anglesey, LL77 7TW; tel: 01248 752564

YSTRADGYNLAIS
The Register Office, County Council Offices, Trawsffordd,
Ystradgynlais, Powys, SA9 1BS; tel: 01639 845104

Appendix 4

Surviving Welsh Census Returns
1801–31

ANGLESEY
1801 Amlwch, Llannerchymedd and Llanwenllwyo (UCNW, Bangor
Mss 1488)
1821 Beaumaris (UCNW, Beaumaris and Anglesey Mss 2/19–20)

BRECONSHIRE
No relevant material available

CAERNARFONSHIRE
No relevant material available

CARDIGANSHIRE
1821 Llandygwydd (Pembrokeshire Archives, Parish Record No. 10)

CARMARTHENSHIRE
1821 Llanarthney (Carmarthenshire Archives, CPR/35/43)

DENBIGHSHIRE
1811 Clocaenog (Denbighshire Record Office PD/20/1/46)
1821 Gresford (Allington, Marford, Hoseley townships only)
(Denbighshire Record Office, PD/34/1/323)
1821 Henllan (Denbighshire Record Office, PD/38/1/315)

FLINTSHIRE
1811 Mold (Flintshire Record Office, D/KK/145)
1821, 1831 Northop (Flintshire Record Office, P/45/1/201-2)

1831 Mold Llwynegrin township only (Flintshire Record Office, P/40/1/58)

GLAMORGANSHIRE
No relevant material available

MERIONETHSHIRE
No relevant material available

MONMOUTHSHIRE
No relevant material available

MONTGOMERYSHIRE
1831 Penstrowed (Powys County Archives Office, Parish Record No. 3)

PEMBROKESHIRE
No relevant material available

RADNORSHIRE
No relevant material available

Appendix 5

Missing and Incomplete Census Returns for Wales

1841
BRECONSHIRE
Llanhamlach (Lower Division)
Vainor

DENBIGHSHIRE
Clocaenog
Derwen
Llanarmon

Llanelidan
Llanfair-Dyffrin-Clwyd

FLINTSHIRE
Bangor (part)
Erbistock
Gresford(part)
Hope or Estyn
Llanarmon (part)

Malpas (part)
Threapwood
Worthenbury
Wrexham (part)

GLAMORGANSHIRE
Cowbridge
Llanblethian

Merthyr Tydfil
St Bride Major

1861
BRECKNOCKSHIRE
Brecknock, St David
Glynfach

Hay
Llanigon

CAERNARFONSHIRE

Caernarfon
Deneio
Llanbeblig
Llanfaglan

Llannor
Penrhos
Pwllheli

CARDIGANSHIRE

Aberystwyth
Broncastellan
Cellan
Clarach
Dihewid
Fforest
Henllan
Issayndre
Llanbadarnfawr

Llanddeiniol
Llandyssil
Llanfairclydogau
Llanycrwys
Mynachty
Nantcwnlle
Pencarreg
Uchayndre
Vainor, Upper and Lower

CARMARTHENSHIRE

Abernant
Laugharne
Llandawke
Llandebie
Llandilo Town

Llangunnock
Llanllawddog
Llansadwrn
Merthyr
St Clear's

DENBIGHSHIRE

Bettws yn rhos
Bodfary
Derwen
Dremeirchion
Dyserth
Efenechtyd
Erbistock
Henllan

Llanddulas
Llanefydd
Llanelidan
Llanfair Dyffryn Clwyd
Llanrwst
Meriadog
St George

FLINTSHIRE

Arddynwent
Caerfallwch
Cefyn
Cilcen
Golftyn
Gwaenysgor
Gwernafield
Gwysaney
Hartsheath
Hendrebiffa
Holywell
Kelsterton
Leadbrook, Major and Minor

Leeswood
Llysdanhunedd
Llysycoed
Maesygroes
Mechlas
Mold
Nerquis
Northop
Rhesycae
Soughton and Connah's Quay
Tre-llan
Trellynian
Wepre

GLAMORGANSHIRE

Ewenny
Laleston
Lower Thytheston

Merthyr Mawr
 Donats

MERIONETHSHIRE

Llanelltyd
Llanfachreth

Llangower

MONMOUTHSHIRE

Bettws
Caerleon
Goldcliff
Henllis
Kemeys Inferior
Llangattock
Llanhennock
Llanmartin
Llanvedw
Llanvihangel Llantarnam
Machen, Upper and Lower

Malpas
Mamhilad
Michaelstone y Vedw
Nash
Redwick
Rhydygwern
Risca
Skenfreth
St Woollos,
Tredunnock
Whitson

MONTGOMERYSHIRE

Chirbury
Guilsfield
Llanarmon Mynydd Mawr

Llanfyllin
Llansanffraid: Pool Deythur

PEMBROKESHIRE

Caldy and St Margarets Islands
Castle Dyrran
Crinow
Haroldston St Issells
Hasguard
Haverfordwest, St Martin and
  Prendegast
Haverfordwest, St Mary

Haverfordwest,
Llanfallteg
Llanfihangel Penbedw
Nevern
Newport
St Bride's

Uzmaston

RADNORSHIRE

New Radnor
Radnor

1871

BRECONSHIRE

Grwyne – fawr
Grwyne – fechan

Talgarth

GLAMORGAN

Knelston
Llanddewy
Llandilotalybont
Llangyfelach
Nicholaston
Oxwich

Penderry
Penmaen
Penrice
Porteynon
Reynoldston

Appendix 6

Welsh Probate Registries

CARDIFF PROBATE REGISTRY OF WALES
3rd Floor
Cardiff Magistrates Court
Fitzalan Place
Cardiff
South Wales
CF24 0RZ

Email enquiries: cardiffdprenquiries@hmcts.gsi.gov.uk
Tel. enquiries: 029 2047 4373
Fax: 029 2045 6411
Probate helpline: 0300 123 1072

PROBATE SUB-REGISTRIES:
CAERNARFON PROBATE SUB-REGISTRY
The Criminal Justice Centre
Llanberis Road
Caernarfon
Gwynedd
LL55 2DF

Written enquiries should be sent to:
Cardiff Probate Registry of Wales (details as above)

CARMARTHEN PROBATE SUB-REGISTRY
Carmarthen Hearing Centre
Hill House: Picton Terrace

Carmarthen
Carmarthenshire
SA31 3BT

Email enquiries: carmarthenpsr@hmcts.gsi.gov.uk
Tel. enquiries: 01267 226781
Probate helpline: 0300 123 1072

Appendix 7

Post-1834 Poor Law Unions in Wales (showing year of formation)

ANGLESEY
Anglesey 1852
Holyhead 1837

BRECONSHIRE
Brecknock 1836
Builth 1837
Crickhowell 1836
Hay 1836

CAERNARFONSHIRE
Bangor and Beaumaris 1837
Caernarfon 1837
Conway 1837
Pwllheli 1837

CARDIGANSHIRE
Aberayron 1837
Aberystwyth 1837
Cardigan 1837
Lampeter 1837
Tregaron 1837

CARMARTHENSHIRE
Carmarthen 1836
Llandilo Fawr 1836

Llandovery 1836
Llanelly 1836
Newcastle in Emlyn 1837

DENBIGHSHIRE
Llanrwst 1837
Ruthin 1837
Wrexham 1837

FLINTSHIRE
Hawarden 1853
Holywell 1837
St Asaph 1837

GLAMORGAN
Bridgend and Cowbridge 183
Cardiff 1836
Gower 1857
Merthyr Tydfil 1836
Neath 1836
Pontardawe 1875
Pontypridd 1862
Swansea 1836

MERIONETHSHIRE
Bala 1837

Corwen 1837
Dolgelly 1837
Ffestiniog 1837

MONMOUTHSHIRE
Abergavenny 1836
Bedwellty 1849
Chepstow 1836
Monmouth 1836
Newport 1836
Pontypool 1836

MONTGOMERYSHIRE
Llanfyllin 1837

Machynlleth 1837
Montgomery and Pool 1837
(later Forden 1870)
Newtown and Llanidloes 1837

PEMBROKESHIRE
Haverfordwest 1837
Narberth 1837
Pembroke 1837

RADNORSHIRE
Knighton 1836
Presteigne 1836
Rhayader 1836

INDEX